John Waters

BY **JOHN G. IVES**

PHOTOGRAPHS BY *f*- STOP FITZGERALD

Thunder's
Mouth
Press

New
York

A BALLIETT & FITZGERALD BOOK

Dedication:

To my wife Kina, who has ridden the roller coaster with me,
always with a perfect sense of balance; to the lanky fellow traveler
who forced me to dust off my pen and changed my life forever
one night over the Atlantic; and to the friends who died over the
years, younger than they deserved to, of drugs and alcohol and
sexually transmitted diseases, and heart ailments and other weird
denouments for weird people we all loved.—JGI

Acknowledgements:

Me mum, me kids, me bro, me dads. Betty and Bill, my Baltimore connection.
Liz Barrett, editoria supremissima. Balliett & Fitzgerald, good lads all.
To John, who has helped more than he had to, and who is as great as everyone
says. And to Pia, Patty, Pat, Sara, Ricki and Rachel for stimulating,
no-holds-barred conversation.—JGI

Thanks, at Thunder's Mouth, to Neil Ortenberg for his vision and faith,
and to Anne Stillwaggon for her guidance and patience; we are also grateful to
Leith Johnson at the Wesleyan University Cinema Archives and to
Colleen Roome for her timely help. And last, but not least, thanks to
Madeleine Morel for performing the marriage.—B&F

Text copyright © 1992
John G. Ives / Balliett & Fitzgerald Inc.
Photographs copyright © 1992 f-stop fitzgerald
Original text and graphics copyright © 1992 John Waters
ALL RIGHTS RESERVED.

First edition.
First printing, 1992.

Published by Thunder's Mouth Press, 54 Green Street,
Suite #4S, New York, NY 10013

Distributed by: Publisher's Group West, 4065 Hollis Street
Emeryville, CA 94608   (800)788-3123

Series editor: f-stop fitzgerald
Editorial director: Will Balliett
Line / copy editor: Elizabeth Barrett
Series book design: Frank Olinsky
Graphic artist: Beatrice Schafroth
Graphic production: Linda Rubes

Ives, John G.
John Waters / by John G. Ives: with photographs by
f-stop Fitzgerald. —1st ed.
p.   cm. — (American Originals)
Includes the author's interviews with John Waters.
Includes bibliographical references and filmography.
ISBN 1-56025-033-X (pbk.): $11.95
1. Waters, John. 1946-   —Criticism and interpretation.
2. Motion picture producers and directors—Maryland—Baltimore—
Interviews. I. Waters, John. 1946-
II. Title.   III. Series.
PN1998.3.W38I94   1992
791.43'0233'092—dc20
92-6202
CIP

CONTENTS

A GARDEN IN BALTIMORE

BY JOHN G. IVES

I

On a hot, beautiful, Baltimore morning a few days before the Fourth of July, I arrived on a small street in a peaceful neighborhood, with a "university" feel to it. I almost missed the gothic-looking stone house, with the recessed windows and numberless door, nestled in a bouquet of woods. When I rang the bell, John Waters opened the door himself, smiling and greeting me as casually as if I had popped by to borrow some lawn chairs for a birthday party.

Inside—seeming slightly apologetic for having taken up such a conventional habitat—the filmmaker took me on his requisite tour. We went from room to room, starting at the top. Although the architecture is unique, with arches and odd little nooks and crannies, the rooms are tastefully furnished, every inch comfortable and congenial, all set off by large posters for such films as Russ Meyer's *Faster, Pussycat! Kill! Kill!* and Elia Kazan's *Baby Doll.*

There are, of course, the bizarre features, widely publicized in most magazine articles about Waters: the little unfinished room in the attic where he keeps the more risque toys; the portraits of child killers; the electric chair from *Female Trouble* which adorns the main foyer; souvenirs from Jim Jones and Charles Manson; and all over the house, little plates of plastic sushi. But the overall ambience of his home is that of a well-read and self-sufficient artist or intellectual. The living room walls are filled with bookcases, and there are many more books in his office, screening room, and bedroom. The office is equipped with all the necessities of modern life: computer, copier, fax machine. And he has a full-time assistant, Colleen Roome.

We toured our way down to a large old-fashioned kitchen that looked well-used, and outside to a flagstone patio facing the woods in back. We carried out cushions for the cast-iron chairs, and sat at a glass-topped, cast-iron table. The air was muggy, the noises from the city mostly distant. The loudest sound was that of the birds, whose singing was our constant background.

Waters, although rather tall, is almost elfin in his features, and in the sly playfulness of his expression. Elegant and charming, he recalls a classic boulevardier of the thirties, but with a twist. A thinly disguised smirk sets off his trademark pencil moustache, his warm eyes sparkle with derision, but he nevertheless exudes the sympathetic demeanor of a father confessor or elder psychiatrist. Many of his friends claim that this aura of patience and worldly wisdom induces one to open one's soul and confess everything.

In this civilized atmosphere over the next few afternoons, we sipped iced tea and talked about the bizarre genesis of his life and tastes, and the strange and wonderful excesses of human perversion that fill his films. John was casual and relaxed, gesturing with his hands and arms to emphasize points, and often bursting into contagious laughter.

II

John Waters is justifiably well known at film festivals around the world (when *Cry-Baby* screened at the Cannes Film Festival, he was greeted with a standing ovation). Like a funky, American, pop incarnation of Bunuel, Godard or Fellini, he has managed to make a series of shockingly memorable statements on film. And he has blazed this singular path, working with nothing but his own ideas and scripts through nine increasingly widely distributed films.

The director is also a familiar figure on the college lecture circuit, and the author of three books, *Shock Value, Crackpot: The Obessions of John Waters*, and *Trash Trio*, the last a collection of screenplays. He is an avid reader with a host of offbeat specializations—for example, he is a student of "extreme Catholic behavior before the Reformation"— who has written dozens of deliciously offbeat and cynical magazine articles on a wide variety of subjects. He is a movie fan and trivia buff, who also nurses a lifelong fascination with criminals, criminology and cult leaders, attends famous trials and has taught English and drama courses in the Maryland prison system. And most of all, to the public, he is a Cult Figure, something which he finds terribly amusing.

The John Ford of the trash aesthetic, at one time labeled the Prince of Puke (or the "Pope of Trash" as William S. Burroughs, author of *Naked Lunch,* once called him), John Waters has created within his body of work an extremely consistent vision based on an oddly successful combination of exaggerated perversity—bordering, particularly in his earlier years, on the truly lewd and disgusting—and high-camp satire of his own background and its cultural icons. His is a world where life's struggles are staged on the battlefields of fashion and taste, and where the hero (or heroine) may be weird but usually wins in the end. And, of course, the good guys in a Waters film more often resemble the bad guys in most films.

Waters insists that what drives his work is and always has been, "What would make me and my friends laugh today?" Although the answer to that question has evolved over the past twenty-five years, the world he has created is consistently driven by a particular trinity: obsession, taboos, and extremes of behavior. Obsession with one's material, he insists, is an absolute prerequisite for a compelling film; violating taboos has been the substance of much of his on-screen shock value; and flaunting extremes—of behavior, dress and language—is the hallmark of his humor. Woven around and throughout this fabric one can find various themes involving religion, sex, violence, and the plight of the "tortured" woman—the latter portrayed most often by Divine, Waters's late friend and leading actor.

John Waters has created situations that are on the edge for most of us, even over the edge. The bizarre figures in most of his films—like the characters created by Chaplin and Keaton—play endless pranks and endure tragicomic disasters. Yet these microcosms of the criminally insane can be extremely compelling, simultaneously satirizing and mirroring the broader realities that shape our lives.

Part of the "escape" of the movies has always been this liberating removal into other worlds, through which we are then eventually returned to our own with fresh eyes. This is the appeal of the fat man and his gunsel in *The Maltese Falcon,* Bogart in *The Petrified Forest,*

Cagney's *The Public Enemy* or even the Marx Brothers. There is a tremendous catharsis in living beyond the norms of society in the chaotic, dangerous, or simply mad lives of these misfits, within the safety of a movie theater. It is, in large part, what defines the magic of the movies.

The difference with Waters is that his worlds have crossed so far over the line into territories previously considered taboo by society that he himself became classified as perverse and "weird." Normal people not only do not behave this way, normal people do not even watch people in movies behaving this way. These people are deviants, blasphemers, and perverts who deliberately flaunt their behavior. They suck each other's toes, they lick each other's houses, they rape each other with crucifixes and basting syringes, they perform fellatio and wear dildos—and to top it off, it is impossible to keep track of what sex everyone is supposed to be!

You cannot watch a John Waters film, at least pre-*Hairspray*, without feeling that if John Wayne, J. Edgar Hoover or even Jimmy Stewart were watching you watching—and laughing—you would be banished from the American Dream forever. And yet it is the truly outrageous nature of Waters's outcasts and their world, that makes both the frowned-upon escape of watching his films that much more seductive, and the release it delivers that much more intense. (Incidentally, it may be more than a coincidence that in an era in which more and more Americans actually do feel banished from the American Dream, mainstream acceptance has finally come to this ultimate outsider.)

Yet a closer examination of his characters reveals another level, a more compassionate underlying theme. In each film, the hero/heroine is someone with a disability to overcome in relation to the outside world. The handicap may be mental illness, ugliness, pathological criminal behavior, or being saddled with a rotten spouse. But the character is able to overcome his (in fact, usually her) disadvantage and turn it into an advantage: Dawn Davenport turns "crime is beauty" into fame (no matter what the price) in *Female Trouble,* while Tracy Turnblad overcomes fatness to become the reigning dance queen in *Hairspray*. The underdog becomes the winner. So, in fact, these weirdos aren't so weird after all. Ironically, they may be easier to identify with than some of film history's less extreme outsiders, because despite their various disabilities, like you and me, they are just trying to get by. At base, Waters has almost an innocent's compassion, a liberating and lasting quality.

While, as a filmmaker, he respects the trick of turning disability to strength, perhaps on another level he sees it as a personal accomplishment; someone who might otherwise have been an outsider in society, he uses his perspective on that position to find humor and make it accessible. Clearly, Waters's favorite actor, Divine, accomplished the same with his own life.

Divine and John Waters remained close friends their entire adult lives. Divine's persona was a key element of the films they made together—"Divine/John Waters vehicles," as Waters calls them. In the course of my interview with John, there was naturally considerable discussion of Divine and his role in the saga of John Waters and his films. And there were several times when some poignant reminder of Divine's death would creep into the conversation. During those brief moments, John would pause, and an almost imperceptible flicker of silent recognition, a missed beat, would slip across his face.

Several members of John's working "family" have died prematurely over the years. But despite the loss of more than one close friend and collaborator, this committed filmmaker remains a man with an incurable sense of humor about life.

He is a highly intelligent and exhilaratingly funny man in his mid-forties, devoted to his art, and sophisticated in the depth of his perceptions. When Waters is working, he leads a kind of hermetic existence, writing screenplays and articles, reading and studying alone at home. The rest of the time, he sees friends and travels. He still has many of the same friends he had twenty years ago and sees or speaks on the phone with several of them on a daily basis. And he makes all his films in his beloved home city, where he continues to pursue his lifelong satirical examination of the "strange behavior of white people in Baltimore."

III

John Waters was born in 1946 in Baltimore, Maryland, and spent his youth in a nearby suburb—Lutherville—where his mother, Pat, watched over the family: John, his brother Steve, and his two sisters, Kathy and Patricia. The Waters family was what John has labeled "upper middle class Roman Catholic." His father, John Waters, Sr., operated a successful commercial fire protection equipment business.

As documented in scores of magazine articles and his own books, even as a young boy, Waters had a curious appetite for the macabre; he staged car accidents with his toys and coaxed his parents to take him to junkyards where he could explore real wrecks. He likes to recall the golden moment when he found real blood on the front seat of a smashed-up car.

John went to secular private school as a child, then to a Catholic high school where he discovered the source of some of his best material and the roots of some of his most obsessive compulsions.

The nuns at Catholic Sunday school inadvertently introduced him to the world of taboo films; each week they produced a list of unacceptable new film releases, which Waters would then immediately go to see. He made a habit of cutting school and sneaking downtown to see these sleazy films: nudist-camp films, foreign "sex" films, low-budget horror films, and slice-and-dice masterpieces by his favorite filmmakers—Russ Meyer, William Castle, and the Kuchar Brothers (George and Mike).

In early high school, Waters decided to become a beatnik. He grew his hair long, wore faded jeans, and spent most of his time getting into trouble with his oldest friend Bonnie (Mary Vivian Pearce). She bleached her hair, crashed parties, stole liquor, and together they danced an obscene dance called the "bodie green" at Catholic Youth Organization functions. Their reputation was so bad that Bonnie's parents forbade her to see him, so she had to make phony dates with "normal" boys, then run off with John as soon as she got out of her parents' sight—a ruse that was eventually used in *Polyester*.

Another of Waters's hell-raising partners was his girlfriend, Mona Montgomery. They became an expert shoplifting team and often ran away together for weekends in New York City, where they watched underground films and explored the downtown scene. When Waters's grandmother bought him an 8-mm camera, Mona stole enough black-and-white film stock for him to make his first movie: *Hag in a Black Leather Jacket*. He was a senior in high school. According to him, the fifteen-minute film cost about thirty dollars to make and was shown publicly only once, at a local coffeehouse.

Then Waters met a pimply-faced girl with a bubble hairdo—Carol Wernig—who introduced him to the group of friends that would become his extended family and repertory company. The first of those new acquaintances was Glenn Milstead, an effeminate boy who was obsessed

John Waters grew up in a middle-class Baltimore family.

with glamorous movie stars. He would go on to be renamed Divine.

Glenn grew up in a relatively traditional middle-class environment; his family lived in the Victorian house where F. Scott Fitzgerald had lived when his wife Zelda was in a nearby mental hospital. But even as a child, Divine engaged in "games" where he played alone with an invisible character and dressed up in women's outfits. He was too weird for his schoolmates; in junior high school, they beat him up so often that he was frequently escorted home from school by local police. All reports suggest that he was an unhappy child; yet he dreamed of one day becoming famous.

By the time he was in high school, Glenn was going out to parties dressed in drag. He spent some time with other drag queens, but he didn't like the orthodoxy of their lifestyle and devised outfits that intentionally mimicked the drag "look." The other drag queens grew resentful of him, sometimes even violent; they felt he was making fun of them, which he was. That rebellious approach would eventually lead to the "drag queen terrorist" persona that made him famous.

Glenn then introduced Waters to David Lochary, a young hairdressing student with silver tresses, and to Pat Moran, who is Waters's closest friend today. Moran had recently divorced and was rediscovering herself with the help of her gay friends. She introduced Waters to Maelcum Soul, a legend in the sleazy East Baltimore bars and beauty salons frequented by this new crowd. Soul was a model and hostess at a bar named Martick's; her look—extreme makeup and wild clothes from thrift shops—exerted a lasting influence on Waters's view of the characters in his films.

It was 1964. Waters and some of his crowd began using marijuana and LSD. When he enrolled at New York University Film School it was, as he readily admits, just an excuse to move to New York, and he rarely attended classes. After a few months, he was expelled for marijuana use and returned to Baltimore and Divine's elaborate parties. He got out of the draft (too skinny), and went to Provincetown, the artists' haven on Cape Cod, for the first time in the summer of 1966 with Mona. There he met a girl named Nancy, who took the name Mink Stole. They all went back to Baltimore, where Mona and Waters stole more film, and Waters made *Roman Candles*—three 8-mm films (which were projected simultaneously) starring Mink Stole, Maelcum Soul, David Lochary and Divine. That was the first production of Dreamland Studios—Waters's bedroom at his parents' house where the film was shot. *Roman Candles* premiered at a local Episcopal church and attracted the hippest Baltimore crowd.

After trying unsuccessfully to make a film called *Dorothy, the Kansas City Pothead*, Waters moved into a loft apartment in a run-down part of Baltimore with Marina Melin, a sexy Swedish artist whom he had met in Provincetown, and another friend. That loft became the new Dreamland Studios (the surviving members of the original group still refer to themselves as Dreamlanders).

Waters then bought a 16-mm camera and shot *Eat Your Makeup* on his parents' front lawn. It starred David Lochary, Maelcum Soul, and Marina Melin (as a kidnapped girl forced to model herself to death), and featured Divine as "Jackie" in a bizarre reenactment of the Kennedy assassination. *Eat Your Makeup* was screened at a local church and ignored by critics. A few weeks after the premiere, Maelcum Soul died.

In 1969, Waters borrowed $2,000 from his father and made his first feature-length film, *Mondo Trasho*, also shot in 16-mm. During the filming, a male cast member was arrested for indecent exposure (for participating in a scene in the film where the actor was hitchhiking in the nude), and the next day Waters and other crew members were also arrested on obscenity charges. After an embarrassing and unpleasant trial—and a lot of valuable publicity—the filming resumed.

At the film's local church premiere, Waters gave away a free dinner at a nearby hamburger joint as a publicity stunt. Cookie Mueller, who had just been released from a mental hospital, won the burger and, of course, became a Dreamlander. Although *Mondo Trasho* was rejected by New York theaters, it was shown as a midnight movie in Los Angeles, where critics had an opportunity to see it. Pauline Kael elevated Waters's movie to cult classic status in a *New Yorker* review of *Satyricon*, when she referred to the great Italian director's film as "Fellini's *Mondo Trasho*."

In 1970, Waters and his Dreamland team made their first film with dialogue—*Multiple Maniacs*—with another $5,000 borrowed from his father. America was in turmoil, and Waters found inspiration in the chaos. In his book, *Shock Value*, he later noted:

"During the late sixties I felt like a fish out of water. As the rest of my generation babbled about peace and love, I stood back, puzzled, and fantasized about the beginning of the 'hate generation.' Woodstock was the last straw. Sitting in the mud with a bunch of naked hippies and their illegitimate children and listening to Joan Baez was hardly my idea of a good time. Violence was this generation's sacrilege, so I wanted to make a film that would glorify carnage and mayhem for laughs."

Although there was no actual distributor for *Multiple Maniacs*, it played in theaters in Baltimore, Los Angeles, San Francisco, and Provincetown, and in small art houses in several other cities. The film's opening in San Francisco brought Waters and Divine to that city, where they discovered a receptive and largely gay audience. Waters's films had yet to reach a broader market, and his friends—Divine in particular—were skeptical that anything would result from their endeavors.

The Dreamland team had added Vincent Peranio, a local artist, who became—and still is—the production designer for all Waters's films. He introduced the director to two actresses, Susan Lowe and Edith Massey; the latter had a role in *Multiple Maniacs* and later starred in many of Waters's films. During that period, the Dreamlanders made another short film (fifteen minutes)—*The Diane Linkletter Story*—featuring Divine as television personality Art Linkletter's daughter, who had died in a freakish LSD-related accident that launched her father on a nationwide anti-drug campaign.

But Waters's turning point came in 1972 when he made *Pink Flamingos*, his film about "the filthiest people alive." Many devotees consider the $10,000 movie to be his definitive masterpiece. Waters speaks about it in less exaggerated terms but states without question that it changed his life. *Pink Flamingos* made so much money that he never had to get a "day" job again. It is still by far the most popular of all of his films.

He made a distribution deal with New Line Cinema, then a fledgling, New York-based art film distributor that had made its first mark by re-releasing *Reefer Madness*, an anti-marijuana movie made in the thirties. *Pink Flamingos* was an instant smash hit as a midnight show at New York's Elgin Theater, and New Line got bookings all over the country. The reviews for *Pink Flamingos* were respectfully ravaging, expressing admiration and disgust in equal doses. Soon, *Mondo Trasho* and *Multiple Maniacs* were also in demand—and Waters's metamorphosis into a cult hero was underway.

Like *Pink Flamingos*, his next two films were also shot in color 16-mm, and blown up to 35-mm for release by New Line. Waters raised $25,000 for *Female Trouble*—a budget that seemed extravagant at the time (1974)—through private financing. Deciding to live alone for the first time since leaving his parents, Waters moved into a large apartment in an old Baltimore building, creating the new Dreamland Studios. He was finally able to shoot a lot of scenes indoors, using sets built by Vincent Peranio. Van Smith, who had been Waters's makeup man since *Multiple Maniacs*, created some of the most bizarre makeup and costume designs ever devised for a movie. The film opened in New York, and was given a real debut by New Line, replete with hired publicists and an advertising campaign.

In 1977, Waters made *Desperate Living*, his only film after *Hag in Black Leather Jacket* without Divine, who he was in a stage play at the time. Also absent was David Lochary, whose sudden death from a drug overdose had stunned the troupe. *Desperate Living* was also the first that was not a Dreamland Production; the $65,000 budget was raised by a limited partnership. Waters's fundraising ability was becoming a significant aspect of his continuing success as a filmmaker.

Finally, in 1981, Waters made his first 35-mm film: *Polyester*. New Line financed the $300,000 budget, allowing the director to hire a more complete crew, while he and the production company developed a consummate marketing gimmick for the film's release: Odorama, a scratch-and-sniff card with various odors keyed to signals in the movie. And Tab Hunter's appearance in *Polyester* as Divine's character's boyfriend initiated the celebrity cast approach that Waters perfected in his later films. (He had previously lured burlesque star Liz Renay to join the cast of *Desperate Living*; she was a celebrity in his mind, if not in the broader sense.)

That same year, his book, *Shock Value*, was published, incorporating several previously published articles and a wealth of new material.

Waters then undertook what would become a protracted—and unsuccessful—attempt to get financial backing for *Flamingos Forever*, a sequel to *Pink Flamingos*. During that time, he also continued to write articles for magazines such as *Rolling Stone*, *American Film* and *National Lampoon*; in 1986, a collection of those stories and some new material was published as *Crackpot: The Obsessions of John Waters*.

Finally, also in 1986, Waters gave up on *Flamingos Forever* and began work on *Hairspray*, a $3 million PG-rated film that was shot in 35-mm and released by New Line in 1988. It was a critical and financial success. The all-star cast included Pia Zadora, Ric Ocasek

Divine (Glenn Milstead) was a versatile actor whose "terrorist drag queen" alter ego became a central reference point in Waters's films.

(from the rock group, The Cars), Sonny Bono and Debbie Harry. It also starred Ricki Lake, a newcomer to John's team, and Divine—in his last role, and the one that many consider his most fully developed—as Lake's heartwarming mother. *Hairspray* was a major mainstream hit, and John Waters had achieved something he had never intentionally sought: respectability.

But he also lost someone he loved very deeply. Two weeks after *Hairspray* was released, Divine died suddenly from complications relating to his obesity, just as he was enjoying the onslaught of interest from legitimate film and theater that had so long eluded him. His death was a tremendous blow—personally and professionally—and Waters has made it clear that no one could ever replace him. The two were almost collaborators in the sense that Divine was a vital component of Waters's films.

After Divine's death in 1988, Waters published *Trash Trio,* which contained the scripts for *Pink Flamingos, Desperate Living,* and *Flamingos Forever.* The book was dedicated to Divine. Now that Divine, Edith Massey, David Lochary, and Cookie Mueller have all died, Waters says that *Flamingos Forever* will never be made.

After *Hairspray,* Hollywood agent Bill Block engineered a deal with Imagine Entertainment—the highly successful production company owned by filmmakers Brian Grazer and Ron Howard, whose hits include *Splash* and *Cocoon*—to make Waters's $10 million juvenile delinquent musical, *Cry-Baby.* It was released in 1990 by Universal Pictures—a long way from handing out flyers for church screenings in Baltimore. The star-studded cast *á la* Waters featured a typically eclectic mix including television heartthrob Johnny Depp, Patty Hearst, Polly Bergen, David Nelson, Iggy Pop, Troy Donahue, and the newest veteran Dreamlander, Ricki Lake. The reviews were mixed, but the film played in more than 1,500 theaters in the United States and was highly successful in foreign markets.

IV

Over the years, with increasing acknowledgment of his work by the literary/film community, respectability has finally begun to creep into John Waters's reputation. His works have been discussed on network television and in *Vanity Fair* and the *New York Times Magazine.* The Museum of Modern Art in New York acquired several of his films, including *Pink Flamingos,* and included his work in its "Bicentennial

Salute to American Humor." In 1985, the Baltimore Museum of Art, a revered institution in the city that John has so long loved and lampooned, held a three-day retrospective of his work. And the Cinema Archives at Wesleyan University in Connecticut houses a major collection of carefully preserved scripts, notes, articles, and other memorabilia documenting Waters's career as a filmmaker.

Ironically, this recognition and "respectability" have now become fodder for the new criticism of John Waters. Many of the same critics who failed to understand his earlier works the first time around now complain that his recent films—*Hairspray* and *Cry-Baby*—are too mild, that Waters has lost the rawness that gave his humor such an edge. Some have even implied that he should go back to making movies like *Pink Flamingos*.

Many of the most talented auteur directors began by taking what may have been subconscious issues and expressing them through extremes of either humor or psychological distortion. The early works of Fellini, Bergman, and Bunuel are filled with examples; Polanski's *Cul-de-Sac* and *The Fearless Vampire Killers* also come to mind. For a young filmmaker with few resources, a head full of wild ideas clamoring to be expressed, and sufficient obsessive drive to accomplish his or her own greatest ambition, extreme expression is often the starting point.

In the middle period of Waters's work—with *Female Trouble*, *Desperate Living*, and *Polyester*—he moved towards increasingly intricate manifestations of his earlier concepts. Then, with *Hairspray* and *Cry-Baby*, he turned in a new direction. Having matured as an individual, made peace with the craziness around him, and recognized the commercial potential of a toned-down version of his film humor, Waters did the only thing he had yet to do: he tackled the mainstream.

Waters saw his PG-rated civil rights comedy, *Hairspray*, as a challenge to capture a broader audience than that of his earlier films. The film worked tremendously well on that count. It also succeeded as a story, as social commentary, and most of all, as humor.

The issue is perhaps more complex with regard to his juvenile-delinquent musical, *Cry-Baby*. Waters's own explanation for the film's relative lack of popularity in America is that he was trying to satirize a specific film genre with which the younger audience—at whom the film was aimed—was not sufficiently familiar. He also points to the loss of Divine, whose presence had always been a built-in subversive focus. Nevertheless, *Cry-Baby* worked well within the musical format and, on a technical level, it far exceeded anything Waters had accomplished before.

In fact, the very act of John Waters making a family film was outrageous. But now that he has accomplished that, he has made it clear that future films will be R-rated, allowing him considerably more freedom of expression.

Beyond that, it is presumptuous, foolish even, to either attempt to "sum up" or predict a man's work when he is still very much in the middle of it.

Is Waters at a crossroads in his career?

Suffice it to say that the John Waters with whom I spent three days probing and analyzing is a more sophisticated and overtly meditative individual than the young man who set out to shock and scandalize an audience of contemporary hippies and gays twenty-five years ago. As to where this will take his work, I leave that to the second section of this book, and then perhaps, if we're lucky, to another conversation, a dozen years hence, in his garden on a quiet street in Baltimore.

ARTIST
IN DIALOGUE

WITH JOHN G. IVES

First Films

JOHN IVES: How did you feel when you first saw your own footage? Was it what you had envisioned?

JOHN WATERS: No. I thought it was going to be black, no image on it. (Laughs.)

IVES: So it was a relief...

WATERS: ...that it turned out at all, that you could see anything. The scene in *Hag in a Black Leather Jacket* where it's double-exposed? That was accidental. I put the same roll of film back in. But people thought it was arty. (Laughs.) I don't even know if you could do that today. When I saw the footage, I thought, "What's this? They gave me somebody else's roll of film." We would shoot whole days on *Pink Flamingos* and it wouldn't turn out, because I didn't know what I was doing. The film jammed and came back with big scratches down the middle of it. I didn't have an editing machine, so I would edit it and then put it back through the projector to look at the cut. Can you imagine? With no work print. The original. *Pink Flamingos* had no work print. To this day I don't know how that's possible. I put it through hundreds of times.

IVES: What about now?

WATERS: I go to dailies every day. [*Dailies are screenings of the visual and audio workprints of each day's shooting, usually held the next day, so the director and others can mark their progress.—JI*] They're torturous. They never look as good as you want. But making a film is always like that to me; the day you think up the idea is the best. Making that *real* is always downhill. It's never as fresh as the day you thought it up. I think it's probably like that for everybody, but you're not supposed to say that.

IVES: Can you picture ever doing anything besides filmmaking?

WATERS: Yeah. Writing books. But I certainly don't want a career change. I have back-up things, but the only time I think of them is when I can't make a movie, for some reason. Then I think about writing—journalism or books. But if you mean suddenly saying, "Oh, I'd love to give all this up," no. I don't ever have that fantasy. What would I do? Maybe open a bookstore when I'm real old—a really good one where you didn't have to make money or anything. You'd just have the best books, and you could be mean to customers.

> *The day you think up the idea is always the best. Making it real is always downhill.*

IVES: I'd open a movie theater again. Go back to Provincetown, dust off the doors. But that was a tough business. You had to convince people who came down from Montreal in pedal-pushers to look at scenic New England to come in and see *Now, Voyager* or *Pink Flamingos*...

WATERS: ...to go into a movie theater when they might be missing valuable drinking time. I used to hand out flyers when I rented the Art Theater [in Provincetown, to show the films] and when we showed them [in Baltimore] in churches. The Provincetown Bookshop would give me the whole window and I'd turn it into a billboard. And we would go out in costume and hand out all the flyers for two weeks. When it was in the Art Theater, I had to guarantee my percentage of every seat. If nobody came, I'd owe thousands of dollars.

IVES: Did you make it?

WATERS: Oh, it was sold out every time. He [the owner] was sort of astonished. The cast and I really went out and worked to sell it. For *Eat Your Makeup*—that was shown in the church—we gave out candy lipstick. And we did all sorts of promotion. You have to do that. We used to give away door prizes, like to the worst restaurant in town. You'd get a dinner for two at The Doggie Diner. We did that in San Francisco.

IVES: Isn't that how you met Cookie [Mueller]?

WATERS: Yes. That was the Little Tavern in Baltimore.

IVES: Tell me about when you first went to New York.

UNDERGROUND FILM PREMIERE

★ ★ ★ ★ ★ ★

DREAMLAND PRESENTS
John Waters' new film
EAT YOUR MAKEUP

Starring Maelcum Soul, David Lochary
and introducing Marina Melin

with bob skidmore/diving judy boutin/
bonnie pearce/extreme unction/howard gruber/
and the child star Lizzy Temple Black

"The story of a deranged governess and
her lover who kidnap models and
force them to eat their makeup
and model themselves to death"

TWO NIGHTS ONLY !!
Fri + Sat. Feb 23rd + 24th
8 and 10 P.M.
Great Hall- Emmanuel Church
Cathedral and Read Sts
Donation 99¢

ALSO
"Short Circuit" by the 8 yr. old
DAVID WISE
"bits and moments of free creative
expression.... a small wonderland"
Jonas Mekas, Village Voice

Hand-written flyer for *Eat Your Makeup*, a 1967 film which featured a
Waters-style re-enactment of the John F. Kennedy assassination.

WATERS: Before NYU, I would run away from high school and go there.

IVES: And you discovered this new world and underground films and all those strange people.

WATERS: Well, I had already discovered the world I was looking for in downtown Baltimore in a bar called Martick's where Maelcum Soul worked. It was a very mixed crowd—bohemians, beatniks, drag queens, and people that I had read about in [William S.] Burroughs and John Rechy and Tennessee Williams. So when I first went to New York, I had already been hanging out downtown; I didn't ever hang around the people I went to high school with by then. I just hooked school, got caught—I didn't care about it. I took LSD in high school; 1964 was the first time.

IVES: There weren't many people taking it then.

WATERS: No, they hadn't even heard of it. They had it here [in Baltimore] at the mental hospital—Sandoz acid—and we knew people who stole it. I used to go to New York with Mona [Montgomery], but we had no money. Every week we'd have to think, "How are we gonna get money to go?" Also, we weren't allowed to go, so I would type up fake permission slips for her to go on a sorority weekend. She wasn't even in a sorority, but the permission slips looked so official that her mother would sign them and give her money to go. (Laughs.) Once she hocked her brother's stamp collection, which, when I look back on it, was a horrible thing to do. We thought nothing of doing stuff like that, then. We would hitchhike in Manhattan, which nobody did—even in the sixties. And we would have nowhere to stay. We'd stay at this hotel on Eighth Street—the Earl, maybe—or we would just go up to anyone on the street and ask, "Can we stay with you for the night?" And people said yes! But it was almost normal to do that in the sixties. Sometimes we'd stay with Warhol fringe people who would take amphetamines and listen to Maria Callas all night; we used to take black beauties and do the same thing—we'd go to four or five movies in one day. We'd start out in the morning, and just keep going. I saw Warhol's *Couch* and the films of the Kuchar Brothers, and I also saw a lot of movies at St. Mark's Church.

IVES: Where else were those movies showing?

WATERS: The Bridge, The Gate, Filmmakers' Cinematheque...

IVES: You were sixteen?

WATERS: And seventeen. I made *Hag in a Black Leather Jacket* when

I was a senior in high school. I would go there [to New York] to see all those movies. That's where I saw *Scorpio Rising* [*Directed by Kenneth Anger—JI*], Genet's first movie [*Un Chant d'Amour*], all that stuff. Then I went to NYU. The only reason I went there was so I could live in New York, and I only went to one class. I got expelled. My parents would say, "How's school?" I'd say, "Fine." But I never went once. I lived in the dorm and went to movies every day.

IVES: You've said that world sort of changed your life. Did you meet other filmmakers?

WATERS: No. I went and watched the movies with my friends and came back [to Baltimore] and tried to make them. At the same time, we'd go to the drive-in every night here, which was a completely different influence. But [going to New York] gave me the idea of what I wanted to do as a career; I realized that it was possible. The Theater of the Ridiculous was really popular then. That was an influence on me, too. And Samuel Beckett's *Waiting for Godot*, and LeRoi Jones's plays, and Jack Gelber...all that stuff. We used to go to theater all the time. I was obsessed by all that stuff. And we read all the time, too. I always worked in bookstores.

IVES: Did you read about film?

WATERS: Yeah, I read *Film Culture* and the *Village Voice*. The *Voice* had Jonas Mekas's column every week. I loved him, because he wrote about people I wanted to know about. Those were the two main papers that wrote about underground movies then. Then later—much later—I read *Film Comment*.

IVES: You didn't read James Agee, or any of that?

WATERS: Oh, no, no. I liked Parker Tyler. He was my favorite critic. He wrote a book I loved called *Underground Film*. He was a really insane film person. I wanted him to write about my early films, so I called him—he was very old and dying—and he said (imitates an old man's shaky voice), "I'd like to, but I'm too sick." I would just call people up like that. They were all older than me.... By the time I was twenty, I was already making *Mondo Trasho*. I really went from puppet shows to making movies; there wasn't much time in between.... It was too mortifying to be a puppeteer. It was so uncool, I would never tell anybody; I was too embarrassed. But I was used to making the money. When I was a kid it was great, when I was a teen-ager it was really embarrassing.

IVES: Did you write the stories?

WATERS: They were just "Cinderella" and "Punch and Judy" basically, and then I got so bored with it that I would try out things, and the children would just look at me—confused. You know, it wasn't that they were upset. It was just, "Huh?" Then I realized I'd better get another job. (Laughs.) But when I was making those early movies, I worked for a famous survey company for a while, not for long.

IVES: Movie surveys?

WATERS: No. You'd [go to people's houses and] give them magazines with fake ads and then go back the next day and ask them two-and-a-half hours of questions about what they remembered. But the problem was, no one would ever let me in the house, because I had real long hair and looked weird, so I made up every one of the answers. I had to be so many different people; it was really a good way to develop characters. I never got caught, so I think they believed them.

IVES: So you never completed any real questionnaires?

WATERS: No housewives ever let me in. And then—this was really rude—Bonnie used to send away for the whole UNICEF kit, and she'd get dressed up really straight and collect money, and we'd buy LSD with it. All that kind of rip-off shit was politically correct then, which is really hard to imagine now. That was the main thing that really upset my parents when *Shock Value* came out. They said, "We never knew you stole." To them that was really appalling, and now I get why. (Laughs.) But then it was how most of the people I knew lived, because no one had real jobs. I mean, fake credit card phone calls, doubling your traveler's checks every time you moved to a new city—we always did that. (Laughs.) The *Berkeley Barb* printed the new codes so you could just make up a new credit card number every time, and it always worked. Can you imagine that? I think back on that, and it's really very strange that it was completely accepted. I used to call New Line [*New Line Cinema, a film distributor based in New York, which distributed all of Waters's films except the first three and* Cry-Baby.—*JI*] on them [fake credit card numbers], and everybody there knew it. I mean, can you imagine that, making business calls on a phony credit card to your distributor? I knew then New Line was the perfect distribution company for me.

IVES: You mentioned watching Warhol's films on your trips to New York.

WATERS: Warhol's influence on me was giving me the confidence that I could do it [make films] with my friends, for no money. But I didn't want to do things like filming just one person doing something. Who influenced me most was the Kuchar Brothers [George and Mike], because their films were lurid melodramas.

IVES: Which films?

WATERS: *Sins of the Fleshapoids, Hold Me While I'm Naked, Pussy on a Hot Tin Roof.* They made 8-mm movies that showed at the Cinematheque. And they made a lot of their movies in Co-op City [in the Bronx], which I loved. So those movies, along with Russ Meyer and trashy Herschell Gordon Lewis gore movies, were a stronger influence than Warhol. And Kenneth Anger was a huge influence. All put together, it was the New York underground school meets the drive-in movies, with Ingmar Bergman giving them some fervent angst. *Hour of the Wolf* was a huge influence. But the real underground movie scene only lasted a couple of years.

> *It was the New York Underground school meets the drive-in movies, with Bergman giving them some fervent angst.*

IVES: And there's no underground film equivalent today?

WATERS: There was a punk scene that had Richard Kern's movies, which I liked very, very much. I liked Nick Zedd, Richard Kern, all those punk filmmakers who showed their films when punk came out at the Kitchen and everything. They didn't at all get the notoriety and publicity that underground films got, but that's the only thing that's been at all like that [New York underground] scene. And they were all quite defiant and quite junk-ridden. But what happens today is that a good underground movie gets picked up and you have to spend all the money to open it just like you do with any other movie. That's the difference. In the underground movie scene, you just put one little ad in the *Village Voice*, and everybody knew about it and went. That doesn't work anymore.

IVES: What would somebody do today if they were inspired to make cheap movies?

WATERS: Unfortunately, they all make videos today. Video is the 8-mm of today. Anybody can make video today, you know? The fact that it used to be hard to get your hands on the film equipment made it worthwhile only if you really wanted to make films. Now everyone can get their hands on the video equipment; they just want to do it because they think it'll make them cool or get them

ATTENTION
PARENTS !!!

As of the first of April, John WATERS will return by demand to giving inexpensive Top Rate puppet shows for children's parties, church groups etc., after a 1½ year temporary retirement due to school obligations. A standard in this field for over six years, an all new improved show will be offered for the same EARTH!! BANG !*! SHATTERINGLY BOOM POW low prices that have kept Mr. WATERS in constant demand for years!!!

FOR INFORMATION call CL20392

The consummate showman, Waters first used his keen talent for promotion to hype his puppet shows.

laid more or something. I still think you could do it [make a film cheaply], but there is no movement. When *Pink Flamingos* became a hit, that movement was long gone. All those movie theaters were closed. The Elgin was it, because of *El Topo*—the first midnight movie. That's when midnight movies became what the underground movie scene used to be.

IVES: What about San Francisco? That was an influence on you also, right?

WATERS: Yes, because that was the first place our films caught on, outside of Baltimore. I didn't know a soul there. I lived in my car when I first got there.

IVES: When was this?

WATERS: This was in 1970. I left Provincetown and went there.

IVES: So you had already been making films for a few years by then.

WATERS: Oh, yeah. I had already made *Mondo Trasho* and *Multiple Maniacs*. There was this scene going on at the Palace Theater. A big scene. I mean, Gore Vidal and Truman Capote would be there to see the Cockette shows. The audience was half the show. Everyone was on LSD. It was quite debauched. But straight people went too—not a lot—

Divine never believed anything was ever going to become of any of this.

but it was insanity San Francisco-style, and it was really good. A guy named Sebastian ran it, he was the booker. He had the Palace Theater, and later a place called the Secret Cinema, which was a movie theater in a loft—it was great. He showed *Multiple Maniacs* at both, and the audience went nuts for it. They all went nuts for Divine. So Sebastian said, "Let's fly Divine here." Before that, Divine never believed anything was ever going to become of any of this. He was in Provincetown without one penny, and now Sebastian was sending him an airline ticket, which was really a big deal for us then. I said [to Van Smith], "Do something weird with his hair." So Van shaved off the front of Divine's hairline, got him in drag, and put him on the airplane. He flew alone on that airplane—in full drag—without a penny in his pocket. When he got off the airplane [in San Francisco], all the Cockettes were waiting for him at the airport—in costume. It was a huge arrival.... He [Sebastian] wanted to introduce Divine [at the film showings] so we did stage shows that I wrote, you know, where Divine would come out pushing a shopping cart and throwing dead mackerels into the audience. We always used to do that before people in the audience had expensive clothes. (Laughs.) And I wrote him a show once that was very similar to the nightclub act he did in *Female Trouble*. He ripped telephone books in half, he threw fish, he did all that. We did the act other places, too, like at colleges. We always had a stolen cop uniform we'd bring with us, and get some hippie to play the cop. At the end of the act, the fake cop would come on stage and Divine would kill him. That was nice; the audience loved that.... I don't think audiences had really seen a psychotic drag queen who wasn't trying to be like pretty, who was being sort of a terrorist. He used to do speeches I wrote, saying, "I came to California; I watched and I waited, and I killed people's pets." Before they caught Charles Manson, we used to say that Divine killed Sharon Tate; that was part of his act. People would be like, "*Auggggh*."

IVES: What movie was that in?

WATERS: He said it in *Multiple Maniacs*, but then halfway through [filming the movie] they caught him [Manson], so I had to change the end. But when we were touring, Divine would say, "I did it," and people thought maybe he did. I mean, they weren't quite sure. And I used to write that he followed hippie couples to their apartment, waited outside their window eating white sugar and watching their pets, and then one by one he killed their pets, and then them. That was punk, before there was such a thing. It really caught on there [San Francisco] way before New York. I went back to Baltimore and made *Pink Flamingos*, and then we came back to San Francisco. New Line kept it [the unreleased *Pink Flamingos*] for a year, so I was penniless. I moved to New Orleans and waited for *Pink Flamingos* to come out. [And] New Line didn't distribute the old ones yet—they wouldn't. So I would go out and try to get the old ones shown. And I traveled around the country with them. I did it in Isla Vista, California—remember, that's where they burned a Bank of America building.

IVES: Right. That's why you picked that place.

WATERS: (Laughs.) I loved that community. I was there for a while. I also stayed with the curator of the Santa Barbara Museum, Ron Cuchta, who married Mink Stole's [a.k.a. Nancy Stoll] sister, Sique. I didn't really rough it too much. They had this beautiful house, and I would go to these society parties with them. I had two lives. So did they. I've always liked both of those lives.

IVES: Did that trip, and being in San Francisco, influence your film-making?

WATERS: No, but it certainly influenced Divine's popularity.

IVES: Did you meet other people who were making films there?

WATERS: I was in a show business community there, yes, with the Cockettes and Sebastian. And a lot of the people who worked with me came to live out there, too. Mink lived out there for a time. Bonnie [*Mary Vivian Pearce, one of Waters's oldest friends—JI*] hitch-hiked, by herself, from New Orleans to San Francisco—in high heels. And nothing happened to her, she got rides the whole way. (Laughs.) So a lot of us were out there, but then we'd always come back here [to Baltimore] to make movies, and then go away again. I used to travel with a car full [of stuff]. I even took my crucifixes with me. I had electric crucifixes. I traveled with furniture, like a gypsy, you know, I lived in that car. I drove back and forth across the country, all five major routes. I mean, I did *On the Road* to death. But David Lochary had long silver-dyed hair, and it was really scary to get out [of the car] in some of those [small] communities. We'd go into an Arizona truck stop to get coffee, with David's silver hair with the roots purposely shaped in a perfect heart. I had really long hair and we wore shiny shirts and pimp-looking outfits or cowboy shirts with padded guitars on them—purposely hideous clothes that we bought in thrift stores. But we didn't wear hippie shit. We liked black pimp-wear, to make us look scarier. (Laughs.) Then I went to L.A. to go to the Manson trial. That was the very first time I ever went there. *Multiple Maniacs* played there and got a really good review in the L.A. *Free Press;* it did great. I loved L.A. the minute I got there, because it looked exactly like what I always thought it would look like. And whole streets smelled like film, where all those labs were.

IVES: But you didn't want to live there?

WATERS: Oh, I *never* want to live there, but I still like to go to Los Angeles a lot. Every day I would hitchhike to the Manson trial and spend the whole day. Usually somebody from the trial would give me a ride home, some lunatic who also spent their whole day at the Manson trial.

But, San Francisco was the first place I got any real recognition before *Pink Flamingos.* Then *Multiple Maniacs* was picked up by the Art Theatre Guild, by this guy named Mike Getz—he had a thing called Underground Cinema 16—and it played in maybe forty cities at the peak. I gave him a print for forty weeks, and I got a dollar a minute every time they played. It was great; I got ninety dollars a week. Ninety dollars then was maybe like five hundred today.

JOHN IVES: Did it make you want to rush out and make longer films? A three-hour epic?

WATERS: No, my films were already way too long. But they played in every major city—at midnight—once. They were very well supported, really. That was all before *Pink Flamingos* became a hit. Then everything changed completely. It played in every theater I'd been trying to get in before and never

> *After Pink Flamingos became a hit everything changed completely. I got into theaters I could never get into before.*

could, and it played for years at some places...almost ten years in L.A., at the Nuart.

IVES: And then they played your other films, too.

WATERS: Just *Mondo Trasho* and *Multiple Maniacs*. The ones before were never distributed. They had separate sound tracks on tape that were impossible to synchronize. Even when I put them on video—which I finally did just for myself—they're not exactly right, the sound, because it was twenty years ago. I remember the torture of doing that, of thinking that I could synch a whole movie with a tape. You know, different projectors run at slightly different speeds—a tiny bit threw the whole thing off because it was closely synchronized. Those films remind me of all these shots now in *JFK*. We did the whole Kennedy assassination in 1967 with Jackie, the exact same shot I saw in *People* magazine. [People *magazine ran a cover shot from the original Zapruder film showing President Kennedy being shot, which Oliver Stone recreated for* JFK *and which Waters had re-created much earlier for* Eat Your Makeup.—*JI*]

IVES: Stone probably saw your film....

WATERS: No, he didn't. He didn't see *Eat Your Makeup*, because that only showed a few places. But I look at those shots and I think, "I have a shot right upstairs that's like that." It's the same shot. I have to get to some magazine to dispute his claim of being the first person to do the Kennedy assassination. He waited so long! We did it almost the next year! It really made people so uptight at the time, I mean, it was really worse than blasphemy—which we did next. I showed Willem [Dafoe] the rosary job from

OFFICE OF THE MARICOPA COUNTY ATTORNEY

101 W. JEFFERSON STREET, SUITE 400
PHOENIX, ARIZONA 85003

~~(602) 262-3411~~

261-5831

TOM COLLINS, COUNTY ATTORNEY	NORMAN C. KEYT, CHIEF DEPUTY

January 24, 1985

YOUR TAX DOLLARS AT WORK

Valley Art Theater
509 South Mill
Tempe, AZ 85282

To Whom It May Concern:

Your ad in the January 23-29, 1985, issue of the New-Times indicates that on Friday and Saturday nights, January 25 and 26, you are showing a film entitled "Pink Flamingo".

That film was seized in Phoenix by means of a search warrant after a judicial determination that there was probable cause that the film violated Arizona obscenity law. I have attached hereto a copy of the New-Times ad and that portion of the search warrant affidavit describing the film.

Sincerely,

Randy H. Wakefield
Deputy County Attorney

RW/mh
Enc.

SORRY NO PINK FLAMINGO

"Your tax dollars at work." Waters's hallmark film, Pink Flamingos, is still considered obscene by government censors in some states.

Multiple Maniacs after he made *The Last Temptation of Christ*. [*The "rosary job" was a scene in* Multiple Maniacs *in which Divine was seduced in a church by a lesbian, played by Mink Stole, who used a rosary as a dildo.—JI*] He was appalled by it. Actually, he laughed. I said, "Imagine if they had seen this? You think they were uptight about *The Last Temptation*, which was so reverent, really? Imagine if they had gotten a load of this!"

IVES: I guess since your early films weren't as widely distributed, you didn't really get much of an uproar.

WATERS: We did with *Pink Flamingos*. It's still legally obscene on Long Island. Can't play there. It got busted in Hicksville, New York, and found guilty. It just got busted in Florida. It got busted in lots of places. In Europe, too. Even today, it's censored in London. The version of it that you can get on video is censored. I had big censorship problems here in Baltimore when they used to have the Censor Board. But there were no laws that said you couldn't eat shit. They didn't have that on the books, so they couldn't bust it because the Supreme Court hadn't ruled whether it was obscene to eat dog shit.

IVES: Yeah, but there were other things in there...

WATERS: ...that they cut. You see, what they usually cut was the chickens...

IVES: ...the blow job...

WATERS: ...the blow job. And sometimes the singing asshole, and sometimes the artificial insemination, which is the most obscene shot in the movie.

IVES: In a moral sense?

WATERS: No, it's the ugliest.

IVES: I think some people would argue that the asshole scene is the ugliest.

WATERS: Why? That's joyous! This is not joyous; this is somebody jerks off in their hand and then sucks it up with a turkey baster and shoves it up a—may I add now—a double of the actress's vagina. (The real actress wouldn't do it.) But I had enough censorship problems. We usually lost, because in an underground movie theater at midnight or whatever time, the audience was very "up" watching it. You know, it was a joyful experience. At ten A.M. in a courtroom with twelve jurors who have never met each other and a stern-faced judge...it is obscene. It is obscene, but joyously. But that's a tough shading to convince a jury of in a courtroom. I saw *Taxi Driver* in a courtroom at the Hinckley trial, and it's completely different than watching a movie in a movie theater, believe me. It's a very unfair way to see it.

IVES: The first time I saw *Texas Chainsaw Massacre*, I was running a theater in New York City, and they asked me to check the reels, because it had come out as a sordid underground thriller and they brought it back with this big art campaign after it was adopted by the Museum of Modern Art. I watched it at ten in the morning, and I had never seen anything like it.

WATERS: I felt like that the first time I saw it. I was shocked. But the Museum of Modern Art did the same thing for *Pink Flamingos.* Right in the beginning they asked for a print of it for their private collection. I was so proud. And they had it in their Bicentennial Salute to American Humor. We always tried to use that in court, but the jury was never impressed. But it may have helped us in that other arrests haven't happened. And when it [*Pink Flamingos*] got busted in Florida recently, there was enough of an outcry of people saying, "This is ridiculous," that the prosecutor settled out of court. All the video store had to do was put the film in the adult section with a warning label on it.... A lot of worse stuff could have happened.

IVES: It doesn't bother you that it's in the adult section?

WATERS: Well, I would certainly rather have that than be judged obscene in the State of Florida.... It's dumb in the adult section, but I get it. In a way, I guess, when people rent it they should know vaguely what they're getting. What happened was the exact joke that I used to use in my lectures, saying that I couldn't wait for a family to go in a video shop and say, "Oh, we loved *Hairspray* so much, let's get another John Waters movie." That's exactly what happened. This couple rented *Pink Flamingos* and, they said, got halfway. I know what halfway is—the asshole. And they called some religious group, who sent an undercover cop in—a teen-age girl cadet—so they could not only bust it for obscenity but underage.... I'm glad I ruined that family's night. I'm sure in the long run all of the publicity in Florida just helped me. I'm sure more people rented that movie after it happened.... It's pretty hard these days to get busted. You might get an X, or an NC-17. And an X means the theaters won't play it, so that is censorship. They don't bust it, though. You only get busted with kiddie porn, pissing, or anything like that. And *Pink Flamingos* is on lists by civil libertarians saying, "Don't push it by showing it, you'll get nailed," because of the scatology thing, which basically is a no-no. But juries these days are letting things off way more than they used to, like the 2 Live Crew thing, which is obscene, too. I think it has the right to be there, but it is obscene if you listen to it and if you believe in obscenity the way prudes do who make the laws.

IVES: Do you feel patriotic?

WATERS: Yes, I think America's the best country. Certainly it's the only country where I could have had any of the success I've had, so I do feel patriotic. But not flag waving...that hysteria of patriotism frightens me. But yet...I'm certainly a capitalist, and I'm certainly for the system. I think it is the country where you have the most chance of any country, for some people. If you're born in the projects though, I think your chances are very slim. I don't think that's right, and I'm not for that. That's why I can't wave flags saying we're the best country in the world.

IVES: How would you change that?

WATERS: I can't change it. You know, there's nothing I can do about it. I don't want to be taxed more, either, because I know how they spend my tax money. [Laughs.] I'm honest about it...as soon as you get any money, you become a little more fiscally conservative. That's probably why I stopped taking drugs after I made *Pink Flamingos*.... I used to smoke pot every day, for ten years. And as soon as *Pink Flamingos* became a hit, I never did again.

IVES: Are you a Republican?

WATERS: No, I'm not a Republican at all. And in all my films I try to find what the liberal sacred cow is, because the liberals are the easiest people to offend—although I guess I'm a liberal.

IVES: Maybe that's why you want to offend them?

WATERS: Probably. They're the easiest to offend because everything's okay as long as it's not in their house. And when it enters their life they totally change their tune.

IVES: Is that the definition of a liberal?

WATERS: Yes. That's what I love now, that people my age marched for Martin Luther King and all that, but now their kids want to *be* black. That's how they can rebel—to only listen to rap, and talk black and hang out with only black kids. That makes people my age—liberals—crazy, which I'm all for. That's what these kids should be doing instead of seventies revivals. The seventies were terrible the first time around.

IVES: Were you a rich kid?

WATERS: I was upper middle class. I wasn't a rich kid. I had to work;

my parents didn't give me money. They backed the movies, though. But I paid them back. Is that being a rich kid?

IVES: Is your family an old Baltimore family? I was reading that book about the history of Baltimore families, including the Waters family.

WATERS: You saw that book?

IVES: I brought it to you.

WATERS: I couldn't believe it, I looked through it last night. Yeah, my parents are a little bit like Mrs. Vernon-Williams in *Cry-Baby*. That's the world I grew up in. I went to a very snooty but excellent private grade school, then I went to a public junior high and a terrible Catholic high school. The rest of my brothers and sisters went to all private schools.

IVES: But you didn't want to.

WATERS: No, but I grew up well-off. And the charm school [in *Cry-Baby*] was very much like the cotillion I had to go to as a kid, dancing class and that kind of crap.

IVES: And you hated all that?

WATERS: Yes, I did. It still makes me uptight.

IVES: You hated it because it was boring?

WATERS: It was so boring. Yes. And because you had to be like

The first time I went to East Baltimore—which is where I get that kind of humor, the look of my movies—it completely fascinated me.

everybody else. You know, they all still wear those same pants, same clothes—they've worn them for fifty years. I don't know why Brooks Brothers puts out a new catalogue every year, it's exactly the same. Just stamp a new date on it...

IVES: Does that partially explain why your films are very exotic?

WATERS: It explains that, but you end up a little bit like it. Hey, where'd I move to? Right around the corner, you know?

IVES: Right. But I'm talking about the films. I mean, the films always have exotic people in them.

WATERS: Well, to me the very first time I went to East Baltimore—which is where I get that kind of humor, the look of my movies and everything—it completely fascinated me, because I was raised to look down on that. So I looked up to it. You know, heavily. Obsessively. And made it the whole style that I make movies about. The villains are usually like how I grew up. Oh, as I got older that changed, like Mrs. Vernon-Williams—she gets nice. But in the old days, certainly it was us versus them.

Autobiography

My name is John Waters. I was born in 1946 in Balti-more, but I live now in Lutherville Maryland. I am 10 years old. My birthday is April 22nd I have a rather big family. I have two sisters, Kathy who is five years old and Tricia who is just one. My brother is four years old. Every night he fights and wrestles with me

JOHN WATERS

Page one of Waters's autobiography, handwritten when he was ten years old, in 1957.

IVES: I don't want to get into Baltimore, because you've already talked and written an awful lot about it.

WATERS: I probably get one request a week. I even got a request from a travel agency that wanted to do a whole bus tour, with me as the guide and they would pay me my lecture fee every time I'd do it. It would be a good idea, but no thanks. I mean, taking like tourists to monster bars, that would be so rude. "Look at these hideous people!" (Laughs.) I mean, that would be everything I'm against, you know?

IVES: That would make a funny film.

WATERS: I know. Just barge in to a little bar with six people sitting there: "Here they are!"

IVES: John Waters's Tour of Baltimore.

WATERS: "Look, there's a beehive hairdo!" Some poor person, sitting there having a beer after work. The whole bus letting out.

IVES: How do you go about writing?

WATERS: The characters come to me first, and sort of what it's about. But the real plot doesn't just come to me in a rush—I wish it would. It comes to me between seven in the morning and noon every day, when I get up and do it. And I have a notepad in my car all the time, and I listen to a lot of music.

IVES: Do you get ideas from the music?

WATERS: Yeah. And I go out a lot and visualize and just watch people and that kind of stuff. But basically it always comes from an obsession with some phenomenon that makes me laugh.

IVES: So you start with a character and then do you sit at your desk everyday from seven to twelve?

WATERS: I make notes.... This idea. This joke. This thing. This character. This this. Pages and pages and pages of notes. Then I go through and outline. This is exactly how I do it: I always have to have an exact kind of legal pads from Towson Stationery. They make the brand I like the best. Bic pens, black, like twenty of them. Then a red Bic pen to circle the ideas I like. Then a red pencil to circle the ones I like even more than the red pen. Then I go back to another legal pad. I have a whole book of titles, a whole book of casting, a whole book of who the characters are and what happens with them in the first, second and third acts.... All of my movies are within five minutes of being ninety minutes long. It goes back to three reels, my old 16-mm days, you know? A beginning, a middle, and an end.

IVES: Do you structure all your films that way?

WATERS: Yes.

IVES: Do you always start with a title?

WATERS: Always.

IVES: Did you ever study any of those theories about film writing and structure and all that?

WATERS: No. Once I looked for a book about it and realized I did all that stuff anyway.

IVES: Do you have plot points? I think in a way you do.

WATERS: Yes. You always know immediately who I like and who I don't like in my movies. There's always a war of some kind between two groups of people. The people who win are happy with their neuroses; the people who lose are unhappy with them. The heroes generally lose something in the second act and get it back in the third. That's the way every movie is. They're conventional on that level.

IVES: So you've got your characters and you start just riffing and you come up with ideas...

WATERS: ...about what happens to them or what their argument's about. What are they trying to get that somebody won't let them get?

IVES: And then it works its way into a story.

WATERS: Yes.

IVES: Do you get an ending at some point before you go back and pull the story together?

WATERS: It's always better when you have the ending first, but unfortunately it isn't always the rule for a successful film. I always had the ending of *Cry-Baby*, which I thought was very strong. Then I realized, when it was over, that audiences didn't. So you can never be sure. Just because you know the ending first doesn't mean you're right. The best ending of all was *Pink Flamingos*, because it made the rest of the movie meaningless as to whether people liked it or not. When they left, they had to tell someone about it. It didn't matter what they thought of the rest of the movie when they left.... J. Hoberman [Village Voice *film critic*—*JI*] said it best; he said it sent me to show-business heaven. It was the ultimate hype. And it was the most commercial thing I ever did. People always said to me, "Why don't you make movies like your old uncommercial ones?" But they were wrong—that was the most commercial movie I ever made.... The main financial problem was that when *Pink Flamingos* was a midnight movie, many theaters didn't charge extra for the midnight show. So the theaters ripped you off heavily, because you had no way of knowing who came to which show. New Line watched over it, but it was difficult to count admissions, you know? But I'm not complaining. I haven't had to get a regular job ever since *Pink Flamingos.*

IVES: When you're going through this process of pulling the characters into a story, at some point do you realize that you have a story?

WATERS: Well, you have to be conscious of the story in the beginning, though I like movies where there is no story. Characters are the most important thing to me....

IVES: But your films always have strong stories.

WATERS: They always do. They always have a narrative, because I know that's what audiences care about the most. They're story-driven. That's a word they use a lot in Hollywood today, which I'm thankful for, because *Pink Flamingos* was technically terrible and it's still playing. So it did something right. Nobody's going in there to look at the camera work.

IVES: Do you ever do research?

WATERS: Oh yeah, I do lots of research. On *Cry-Baby* I did lots. The whole reason *Cry-Baby* happened was a murder case in Baltimore that intrigued me. The case is not at all in the movie, but it's about a girl who was murdered, who was a Drape—a Drapette—and it became a big deal, so all the nuns in school would say, "See what happens to Drapettes?" It was really a famous case in Baltimore. And I was doing all this research in the library about the whole Drape style, and then I got all the articles, and that's how *Cry-Baby* began, even though the movie has nothing to do with the murder case. I always do research. I always go to the library. Now Colleen [Roome], my assistant, also goes, but I send her with, "OK, here's what to find." When I did the skinhead movie [*Waters's first version of* Glamourpuss, *the screenplay that he had been trying to get produced at the time of this interview, involved a skinhead plot.—JI*] I had all the skinhead records, I had all their articles and all that.

IVES: You've talked in some of your articles about a kind of general "life" research. You know, going to sleazy bars, beauty parlors, etc.

WATERS: Oh, that. Yeah, I still do that.

IVES: But that's different from actually researching a particular film.

WATERS: Yes. [Researching a film] is going to the library and finding stuff. And then, of course, Vince [Peranio] and Van [Smith] research all the costumes and make-up. I do research on different things that the characters are into, or even about a neighborhood, and stuff like that. It gives me ideas. I might find one sentence that I can use.... If I see a picture of how I want someone to look, I tear it out. I have folders full of stuff like that.

IVES: So research is not only getting facts for a story, but getting feelings and influences that are going to move it in a certain direction?

WATERS: Or to do the opposite of it. To make the humor...sometimes I write it the exact wrong way. I remember when I did an AA meeting in *Polyester*. I talked to all these reformed alcoholics who said, "Why are you asking us?" People who are in AA are pretty serious about it. And I would say, "Well, what happens in AA?..." because I'd never been to an AA meeting. And then they'd tell me all about it, but they would really get nervous because they knew that I'd turn it around and be really mean, like the scene when Divine goes to the meeting, and the alcoholics yell at her, "Say it, say it!" I would say, "No, I'm just curious about it." The whole time I knew that I was going to do the opposite of everything they were telling me. One time we were interviewing all these young girls for a contortionist act for *Cry-Baby*. [*This segment was cut out of the film.—JI*] It was based on a video I have of a real vintage contortionist act from early Baltimore TV, but I realized after we did it, that it could never be as funny as the tape I have. It didn't work because, when we interviewed all these kids, we wanted one who did it sort of badly. And one parent realized that when I said, "Couldn't you do it a little bit not quite as well?" And the parents suddenly got this light bulb over their heads; they got really pissed off and took the kid and stomped out.... Well, they knew who I was, so I think they put two and two together. But that's what I mean. That doesn't work. Something that's so funny in real life because it didn't mean to be—you can never duplicate that kind of humor.

IVES: Your work is always based on humor.

WATERS: Yeah. That's the only thing.

IVES: You would never do a serious film?

WATERS: No. Humor—comedy—can certainly be serious. I think that's the only way you can make a point: get someone to laugh. But am I ever going to make *Interiors*? [*A dramatic film directed by Woody Allen, released in 1978.—JI*] No—although I loved it—because I don't think I'd do it very well. I can't imagine doing a

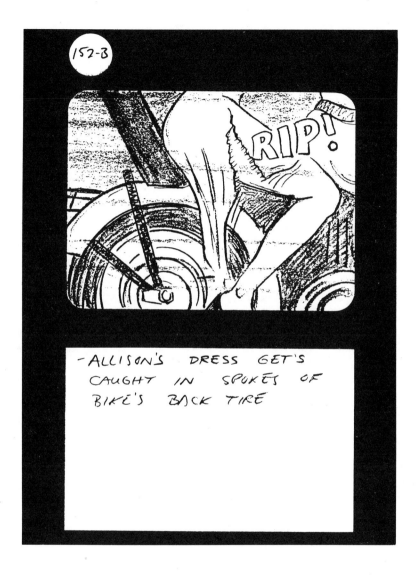

Story board for Cry-Baby.

take and not hoping that the crew laughs.

IVES: It's interesting, though, that you bring up *Interiors*, because you said in one of your books [*Crackpot*] that if that film had been shot in Swedish...

WATERS: They would have loved it.

IVES: ...and done under a *nom de plume*, it would have been taken very seriously by people. Do you ever feel that way about your films?

WATERS: No. I think I've really been understood by the press—except maybe on *Cry-Baby* in a few minor cases. I don't think I've ever been misrepresented or anything.

IVES: Don't you think if *Mondo Trasho* had been done in Italian or German and shot over there that it would have been considered some great expressionist...

WATERS: Not great. No, because *Mondo Trasho* is ninety minutes long; it should have been twenty. It's got twenty minutes of good footage in it. It takes her an hour to get to the bus. The very first time we showed that, people didn't especially like it. They liked *Multiple Maniacs* more, because it had dialogue. It wasn't until *Pink Flamingos* that I knew a movie was going to be a hit from the first night we ever showed it to an audience—when they walked out sort of shocked silly.

IVES: All of these films are outrageous in certain ways, but aren't they also expressions of things that are very serious?

WATERS: Maybe, subconsciously. I didn't sit down before I made *Pink Flamingos* and think, "I'm making a statement on this or that." I just wanted to make a movie that was Bergman, Russ Meyer and drive-in movies put into one. I don't even remember what I thought of when I made that movie. (Laughs.) It was so long ago. We shot it once a week, over a long period of time. The whole script wasn't even done when we started. We did it like a soap opera, basically. I'd write a scene and we'd shoot it. I didn't know the ending in that movie; I knew the eating-shit ending, but I didn't know...

IVES: ...the actual story ending.

WATERS: No. Not when we started shooting.

IVES: What about the earlier ones? Did you know the end? I mean, did you have actual scripts for those films?

WATERS: *Mondo Trasho*, no. *Multiple Maniacs*, yes.

IVES: Aren't the scripts that are in *Trash Trio* taken from the actual films?

WATERS: Yeah...in *Pink Flamingos*, there was a half-hour that was cut out, and I don't have a complete script of that today. You're never going to see the original script published as the final version of a film.

IVES: There's a very distinct story in *Mondo Trasho*.

WATERS: Oh, yeah. And I think it was in my head, and I knew what we were going to shoot every day, but whether I ever wrote the whole thing down, I don't know. When I went through all the stuff and sent everything to Wesleyan, there might have been fragments of it, but I don't think the whole thing was ever written down. [*The Cinema Archives at Wesleyan University in Connecticut, which contain the papers of such figures as Frank Capra, Clint Eastwood and Ingrid Bergman, is the repository of all John Waters's papers.—JI*] I think I just told them, "Okay, today we're gonna..." and everybody basically wore the same costumes through the whole thing.

IVES: Well, you didn't have big problems with continuity and stuff like that because, with the film's undergound look, it wouldn't have mattered.

WATERS: There is continuity in it if you look through it. I mean they have on the right outfits when they come around a corner. (Laughs.) Every Sunday we'd shoot, or something. And we got busted in the middle of it, so that was a big deal. Major deal. [*During the shooting of* Mondo Trasho, *a scene which called for a nude hitchhiker resulted in the arrest of the actor, then Waters and several crew members.—JI*]

IVES: And you had to take weeks off to go to trial.

WATERS: I had to get everybody out [of jail]. There was all this press attention. And then we were scared. But looking back on it, it was kind of exciting when it happened, because we got this national publicity—and it was completely not planned. But my parents were mortified. I was scared to go out and keep filming. We would really look over our shoulders and do it, because we were only about halfway through when it happened.

IVES: Were you shooting in chronological order? I guess so, if you didn't have a script.

WATERS: Yeah. Pretty much, we were. Even *Pink Flamingos* was shot in order—but not completely. I remember doing the whole thing with the singing asshole; we shot him one day with no one there and then filmed the people watching and applauding empty space. I think *Multiple Maniacs* was probably filmed in fairly chronological order, too, because I made it up as we went along.

IVES: So with those early films, including *Pink Flamingos*, you didn't actually use the writing process that you described earlier?

WATERS: No. I didn't do that then.... Before we'd start, I thought up what it was, you know. I knew in *Pink Flamingos* that they lived in a trailer, I knew there were two sides, I knew what it was about. But there was never a complete script that I handed to people before we started shooting the movie. Probably the first third of it was done. And with *Mondo* and *Multiple*, I remember writing the scenes that week and Mink would hand-copy them. We didn't even have xeroxing money. I gave some of them to Wesleyan; some of them are handwritten—they're not even typed.

IVES: Were people improvising at all?

WATERS: No. There was no improvising in *Multiple Maniacs*. In *Mondo Trasho*, I guess I either wrote it down or told them what we were going to do.

IVES: So, afterwards, you put in the voices, her moaning, and all the rap about...

WATERS: ...Jesus...

IVES: ...and the Virgin Mary.

WATERS: That was all done in post-production, at the end, just put over on top of it.

IVES: You didn't know that was going to be in there when they were shooting?

WATERS: Yeah, I did.

IVES: It looked like they were almost mouthing it.

WATERS: Only at the end when Mink's and David Lochary's mothers are gossiping. That's why I had them move their lips silently, with their hands covering their mouths so you couldn't see their exact mouth movement. I knew I was going to dub in *every* dirty expression later on.

IVES: That was great. "Rimmer!"

WATERS: Thanks. Glad you liked it. "Little chicken queen," and "...a Yippie!" (Laughs.) Those films were shot in six days or something...we would do her walking to the bus and the whole shrimp scene in one or two days—and that's forty minutes. [*The opening scene of* Mondo Trasho *involves Mary Vivian Pearce being molested in the park by a man who practices toe-sucking, sometimes called "shrimping."—JI*] The whole mental institution one day, the whole this, whole that—we did a whole lot in one day. But it wasn't continuous. Even *Female Trouble* wasn't shot every day, continuously.

They were never like that until *Polyester*.

IVES: *Polyester* was the first one with a bigger budget. I mean it wasn't a *big* budget....

WATERS: They all seemed like a big budget to us at the time. I mean, when I got twenty-five thousand dollars to make *Female Trouble*, that really seemed like a lot of money to me. And that was the first film we did with A and B editing when you can sort of splice it, that kind of stuff. [*A and B rolls are two or more matching rolls of film, alternating shots and black opaque leader, which, when combined, are used to make a seamless, final release print, with such added lab tricks as dissolves and superimposed titles.—JI*] I had to learn all that.

IVES: You didn't study it anywhere?

WATERS: No. I learned from having to do it.

IVES: How did you learn?

WATERS: Here were my film teachers: Pete Gary, who owned Quality Film Labs, is a very nice man but had big signs in his window during the Vietnam War that said, "Bomb Hanoi." That was what he was like. But it didn't matter. He showed me how to edit and make prints and he got me the people I rented the equipment from, who helped me film and showed me how to do it. *Multiple Maniacs* used that single-system kind of camera that news teams used before video. You couldn't edit easily. The sound went on magnetic stripe right on the film, twenty-four frames away from the picture [*because the sound head was twenty-four frames away from the aperture—JI*], so every cut had to overlap. The sound had to overlap the picture. Pete taught me how to do that. And then another film teacher, Leroy Morais, brought me a bunch of people to crew on *Female Trouble* (Dave Insley, Bob Maier, and Charley Roggero), and they kept working with me from then on. I paid other people to use their equipment that generally was gotten quasi-legally. You know, they had access to the equipment, and maybe the people who owned it didn't know that someone was paying them to use it during off-hours. Like schools. (Laughs.) That's how I learned.

IVES: And you got eight or nine million dollars to make *Cry-Baby*?

WATERS: No, it was eleven. Ten or eleven. Who knows? They put every cent down for every Coke you bought and every film can. So I don't know what the final budget was, but it was certainly way, way, way more than I'd ever had before. But it was also a big movie. I think it would have cost any other director way more than what we spent.

It was a period musical with original music and dancing.

IVES: And pyrotechnics and special effects and people flying through the air and car scenes.

WATERS: Ack! Car scenes, what a drag. They're always the worst to film. They take the longest. That chicken race [in *Cry-Baby*]? I had to sit in that fucking car for a week. One whole week. Every day. They only actually drove a short distance, and we had to get up to speed, to make it with this big camera trucking thirty people around and mikes and everything. Then cut. And you had to drive all the way around and start over to get the next ten seconds of film. In both cars. Then they had to move the car, and in each lap all the cars in the background are set to be going by like in a cartoon going past the same car. So it took forever. And they were on top of a car, singing, so it wasn't...

IVES: Did you use hidden mikes?

WATERS: No, we had playback real loud. And the car wasn't even running, it was on a tow. Not always though. On some of the wide shots it wasn't. And you had to strap them all into all these safety harnesses that were drilled through the roof of the car and then you had to put a baby in the car. You can imagine the Screen Actors Guild rules on that. (Laughs.)

IVES: At least you didn't have to drive far.

WATERS: That's true. I remember those parents looking up just as they handed us their newborn baby to put in the car in the chicken race. (Laughs.) The problem with working with kids is that you can only film them three hours a night. So, you've got to get them there and do their scenes first and if it's in a big scene, how do you do that? You have to shoot...that's why we call them "the cut-away kids." There's not one shot in *Cry-Baby* that isn't a cut-away on the kids. Because you had to film all their scenes first, which was really a pain.

IVES: Will your next budget basically be in the same range?

WATERS: I think the average Hollywood production is something like twenty-two million or so.... My films are still fairly inexpensive, and they do play in every country, which many American comedies don't. Even big ones don't. So it is a brand-name of sorts, which is one reason the studios go for it. I really care about the foreign stuff because sometimes that could make the difference if the film makes money or not.

IVES: Where are you most popular?

WATERS: Through the years, England and Germany were the best,

Vince Peranio's sketch of the Turnblad family's living room for Hairspray (above).
Vince Peranio's sketch of the orphanage for Cry-Baby (below).

but in Australia *Cry-Baby* did great. *Cry-Baby* did better than any of them in Europe.

IVES: That's funny, because in a way it's the most American.

WATERS: And in Paris, they loved *Cry-Baby*. It got rave reviews, because they loved the genre film that it made fun of. They have Johnny Halliday—who is Cry-Baby. But here, the kids who didn't know that genre thought it was corny. They didn't get the joke. Young kids here never saw those Elvis movies. In Paris, they did. They revere that kind of American juvenile delinquent movie.

IVES: Have you ever lived in Paris?

WATERS: Nope. I've been there. They've always been great to me there.... But then, of course, you could always say, "Yeah, but they like Jerry Lewis too." So I wouldn't brag too much. (Laughs.) I certainly love going there when someone else is paying for it and I'm promoting a movie. When you do these foreign trips—and, God knows, Universal was incredibly supportive and I worked hard for them—they sure make it nice for you. I cannot at all say that I had a bad taste of Hollywood with *Cry-Baby*. It was very positive to me. I liked it. And the people were, in some ways, less difficult than some of the people I had to deal with in the past. I've heard lots of horror stories from plenty of directors who work within the studio system, but I guess with me it's almost like the studios know what they're getting if they agree to make a film of mine. The hard thing is getting them to agree to make the movie in the first place. Once they do, I give them what I told them it was going to be. I don't get there and change the whole thing or sneak in stuff that I didn't tell them. I think they were worried about that in the beginning. I remember Sonny Bono was worried about that in *Hairspray*. He said, "Everything that's in the movie is in this script, right?" Like I was going to add a shit-eating scene or something. And I couldn't believe when that happened right when he was running for mayor—and he won while he was playing a segregationist on every movie screen. That's sort of amazing.

IVES: Would you ever make a film in another country?

WATERS: Well, I would hope not, only because I wouldn't know it well

Sonny Bono was worried about Hairspray. He said, 'Everything that's in the movie is in this script, right?'

enough to satirize it well. I've always said I wanted to make a
Baltimore movie that took place around the world, and shoot every
cliche of every country—like the Eiffel Tower—only just shoot it all
here. Most of my stories are very American. When I think of them,
I'd never think of them in another country, to be honest. Even when
I see them in other countries—dubbed—it's amazing to me.

IVES: Would you work outside Baltimore?

WATERS: They always take place here. I mean in my mind they take
place here. But I shot a week of reshoots of *Cry-Baby* in California.
It was fun. I didn't mind it.

IVES: Will your stories continue to be Baltimore-based?

WATERS: Yeah. I think it's expected. I never get hassled about that, that's
part of it. But they could be shot anywhere, really. Most of the time
now we use sets or a location of a house. But it's so hard to make a
movie; I like to at least live in my own house. I ended up being in
L.A. for almost six months with post-production. It's not that I'm difficult about leaving my house. That doesn't bother me. It's just that,
superstitious-wise, I don't think it would be a good idea. Look at what
happened to every director known for working in one country or city
when they left it. It never worked. I'm thinking of obvious ones like
Fassbinder, Bergman. Bergman made that one film in Germany that
was the worst film. I liked it but most people didn't. Fellini never left.

IVES: I don't know if Fellini ever left his backyard.

WATERS: Well, that's what I mean. I like that. Maybe he knew that it
wouldn't work. I could do it, because the humor is a-fish-out-of-
water humor. In Baltimore, the villains are always suburbanites who
are uptight and don't mind their own business. In all my movies.
Every city has that. But I know the extremes of this city best, and
that's what I make movies about—extremes.

IVES: Do you change your scripts in response to what other people
tell you?

WATERS: Well, I listen to what they call their "notes." A good producer
is someone who gives you notes—some of them are good and you
use them—and doesn't make you use the ones that you don't agree
with. And that, so far, is what I've had. Yes, I listen. Sometimes it's
good to listen.

IVES: What about from the studio?

WATERS: I'm talking about the studio. In *Cry-Baby* I certainly had plenty of notes. And I've said this before: It's true they hated it when she

drank the tears, but they didn't make me cut it, because I thought it was really strong. And I said, "Even the people who hate it, it's not going to make them like the movie if I cut it out. And the people who like my movies will like this." And they did. And I certainly had notes with *Hairspray*. Don't think that New Line didn't give you notes. More, probably. I think *Hairspray* is probably a better film from listening to the notes. I at least have an open mind to it. I'm not going to go in and say that no one's opinion is right. But the test...the first two tests are the most horrible things for a filmmaker to go through. That's the most terrifying night, the first night you test it.

IVES: Your films always test now?

WATERS: Well, the last two have, and you can learn a lot from them. But I don't really believe that you can test in Los Angeles. I don't think there are virgins left there to test. They all want to be Roger Ebert. They all want a talk show. And these focus groups? Ack! They keep twelve of them there and this like, shrink, practically, asks them questions. That's when you moan. And you're supposed to sit there and pretend to listen to what they say. Oh, God! We had to go to neighborhoods I never heard of in the [San Fernando] Valley that were so scary—shopping malls that really scared the shit out me. I felt like an old white lady in Harlem.

IVES: You could do the Valley great.

WATERS: Suburbia—that's always my least favorite place, anywhere in the world. That's what I ran from as early as I could, and I've never come back near it. It's my curse, because that's the only place where they want my movies to do better than they do—in deep Mall-Land.

IVES: But a lot of your target is suburbia.

WATERS: Yeah. I have never understood suburbia. To this day, I don't.

IVES: It seems to me that in a way you and [Steven] Spielberg are tackling the same material.

WATERS: In a way. But he loves suburbia, and I don't. I like some of Spielberg's movies, especially *Duel*. I thought that was wonderful. *The Sugarland Express* was a good movie. *Jaws* was a good movie. *E.T.* was a good movie. I'm not against him at all. I like directors who take me into their world, even if I hate their world. Those are always my favorite directors. And their world is almost instantly identifiable as their own. If I didn't see the credits, I could watch it for a while and say, "I know who directed this movie." A lot of them are writers, too. That's the thing, you know.

IVES: *You've* just finished a screenplay....

WATERS: *Glamourpuss.* [*At press-time, Waters's second version of his original screenplay,* Glamourpuss, *which had been picked up by Paramount for "development"—i.e. the process of refining the script and "packaging" it with stars, before making it—had been put in "turnaround," in other words, the studio had decided not to do it. Waters has since made another development deal with another studio, and is in the process of writing that script.—JI*] When I started off, there were two *Glamourpuss*es. Two different plots—one [the first] they all said no to.... I thought up the whole movie, which took a couple of months. Then you have to go in there pitch it, which means you have fifteen minutes to tell the whole story. If they like it, they pay you to write it. When I pitched it, they all said it was really funny but that it was too weird. You know, that they would love to see it but that they didn't want to have anything to do with it. So I went home and thought up a whole new movie. It has the same title, but it's completely different. The one that they said no to was about a white boy who wanted to be black and teamed up with a black fag hag, and together they fought a skinhead invasion of their community. I think it would have been good. I pitched it as *Mahogany Meets The Battle of Algiers* and they laughed right in my face. And one producer, who'll remain nameless, said to me, "John, if I didn't know you I'd think you were insane." And I thought to myself, "You *don't* know me. I've never met you before in my life." I loved pitching it to Dawn Steel at Disney though, because she said, "Oh, well *sure*, when I heard skinheads, I thought Disney!" She knew that they weren't going to do it, but I give an entertaining pitch, so she took the meetings anyway.

IVES: Where did you get the idea for the second version?

WATERS: From the one they all said no to. My original idea was the one they eventually said yes to, but I got sidetracked on this other one, which I sort of always knew was too weird. Maybe I just had to get it out of my system. Maybe I had to think that one up to get to [the second] one, because some of the characters of the first one are in the second one, even though they have nothing to do with the plot. The first one came, I guess, from this thing I wrote for *Newsweek* about how kids should rebel, about being black if you're white—I wanted to make a movie about that. I knew that would be difficult; it's politically incorrect to give a white man a movie to make about black people. That's another reason I wanted to do it.

IVES: I don't think Hollywood believes that white people shouldn't make movies about black stories.

WATERS: I do. It certainly got Norman Jewison away from making *Malcolm X.* Now Spike [Lee]'s directing.... I think it's politically incorrect for a white director to do black movies in the nineties. But it didn't stop me from wanting to do it.

IVES: Did you want to do it because you wanted to do something that you knew people wouldn't want you to do, or did you like the idea?

WATERS: Because it was a rap movie. Rap is the only new music I've liked since 1964. That's why I wanted to do it. She was a superhero fashion model gone insane with machine guns, who sang. But I think they probably didn't want me to do a musical again. It wasn't completely a musical, but it sort of was.

IVES: Why do you like rap?

WATERS: Because it makes me laugh, and it has energy and anger—all the stuff that rock-and-roll had when it first came out. And it gets on white people's nerves.

IVES: This script was more outrageous than some of your more recent stuff, in a way. Were you trying to do that?

WATERS: Yeah, I guess. I have it in my contract that I can make an R-rated movie which, right there, gives me more freedom. It's not shocking anymore for me to make a movie a family can like, so I'm not going to do it again.

IVES: Make a movie that a family can go to?

WATERS: Well, they can go to R-rated movies, but you know what I mean. I can make the humor darker. And I don't mean racially, I mean morally.... The Hollywood thing is very weird, like that I'm there in the first place. In the old days I would have spent two or three years trying to get the money from somewhere else. This time I thought, "I'm not doing that again. Next!"

IVES: So you had to come up with another idea? How did you do that?

WATERS: Well, I had the idea for [the second *Glamourpuss*] when I was making *Cry-Baby.* It's basically about a Hollywood movie star who comes to Baltimore and falls in love with a truck driver.... They like[d] that concept.

IVES: Then you can throw in the skulls on the wall, and the glasses of tears, and the rest of the things....

WATERS: Well, I have a lot of that kind of stuff that I've actually already told them, and they laughed all through it. That's all you've got to do, make them laugh. That's where all my stand-up shit and college lectures come in handy. That's all it is. It's a fifteen-minute stand-up act, a pitch. They don't teach that in film school. [The story] with the movie star is about going through the Hollywood experience, in a way. I like Hollywood, but I also realize that it's almost surreal. And I like it for all the wrong reasons. So I guess that's how this one came for me.... Hollywood in Baltimore. That's what I find funny. It's too easy a target to make an anti-Hollywood movie. This is about somebody who I would like in Hollywood. Who lives there. Who is a Hollywood movie star. How she responds to being in Baltimore... And I guess that comes a little bit from my own experience. Except I'm someone from here who went there and always stayed here. But I certainly saw a lot of people from Hollywood who were here in town for four months while we made *Cry-Baby,* so I know their reaction.

IVES: You mentioned in one of your books that the only film you tried to get a job directing was *A Confederacy of Dunces* [John Kennedy Toole]. Is there other material that you would ever want to do?

WATERS: No. They always want me to. My agent always says, "You know you could make a lot of money if you would direct Hollywood comedies." In my mind, that would be the first time I had to get a job. That's not like working in a bookstore, that's doing somebody else's obsession. That's somebody else's job, and I don't want to do that. I'm not saying that if they were going to take my house away I wouldn't do it, but I don't want to. The other thing is *Confederacy of Dunces;* I don't want to do that anymore, because when a book is so revered by a specific audience, the movie could never be as good as the audience wants it to be. The old maxim may be true: "Good books make bad movies and bad books make good movies."

IVES: What about adapting other people's material? I mean other books. When you read a book, do you ever feel that you'd like to make it into a movie?

WATERS: No, I don't, except there was a book, *A Dangerous Woman* [Mary McGarry Morris], that I liked very, very much. I heard Spielberg had an option on it, which I cannot imagine since it is the grimmest novel I've ever read. But that's the kind of thing I would want to do if I needed work. I loved that book—I mean very, very much. Same with *A Confederacy of Dunces.* I don't know that it would be a hit, but I think that somebody could make a good movie out of it. But I don't really want to do that. The first time I went around and pitched that other movie [the first idea for *Glamourpuss*], they all said no, but they all said, "If he'd direct *this*, we'd be happy to..." I don't even know what it was, because I told my agent, "I don't want to know."

IVES: I'm sure you could make a lot of money.

WATERS: Right. I think I could have directed *King Ralph* or one of those other Hollywood comedies. I didn't see *King Ralph*—maybe it was good, I don't know. But, on a lot of these pictures, too many people wrote them. When eight people are listed as writers, it always makes you think that they're trying to please everybody— which to me means no one will like it. You can't please everybody. Well, some people can. Spielberg doesn't always hit it, but when he does, he does please everybody. I think that's good. I don't have that talent. I don't have it in me to please everybody, because I never wanted to be like everybody else or to please everybody else.

IVES: But doesn't he [Spielberg] go after material that is broad enough to please everybody?

WATERS: Yeah, but he's obsessed with that material in the same way I am with mine. I don't think it's affected, I think it's true. And I think that's why he's very successful with it. He really does love his material. If you don't love your own material, it always shows—and the audience never likes it. You have to get an audience to be obsessed to get them to pay seven dollars to go out of their house and, as Pat Moran's mother said, "sit in the dark somewhere with a bunch of strangers and waste a good outfit." (Laughs.) I always loved that.

IVES: In your earlier movies, were you being more purposely shocking?

WATERS: Not purposely. It was just what my sense of humor was like then. That was in the late sixties when, God knows, everything was more shocking. It was always humor, though—that's what I was thinking of. What would make me and my friends laugh?

I wanted people to be shocked, but to start laughing from the shock. It was joyous shock.

The humor has always, to this day, been based on "what strikes me as funny today?" Then, that stuff did. There were so many taboos left in movies, which there aren't now. Humor was always the first thing. The shock thing, well, it was humor and shock. I wanted people to be shocked, but to start laughing from the shock. Not get angry. Not leave. It was joyous shock. They weren't especially disgusted for real.

IVES: I guess because of the humorous way you approached it, and also the budget level, there was a certain amount of artifice about it.

WATERS: Well, the violence especially. No one believed the gore was real. But it was filmed to look almost like a documentary. I think that was part of the appeal of *Pink Flamingos*.

IVES: And the earlier ones even more.

WATERS: Yeah. That added to that rawness. Raw just means bad. Or primitive and bad. And they were both those things. But people used to think it [the movie] was true. They would ask, "Do you live in a trailer still?" But to be honest, I thought *Pink Flamingos* looked slick compared to what I had just done. Now, I understand it when people start this primitive, blah, blah, blah conversation. It's not primitive to me, but maybe in comparison to some really expensive movie...color for one thing. It gets me how black-and-white now costs about the same as color. It's so rare.

IVES: Try to find a black-and-white television set. They'll think you're crazy.

WATERS: You can just turn your color down. That's why I never understood when people got mad about colorizing movies. If they hate it, turn it to black-and-white. I always said I wished somebody would colorize *Mondo Trasho* and *Multiple Maniacs*—all in green. You know, that puke green.

IVES: So you don't like those movies?

WATERS: Oh yeah, I like them. But I notice all the bad stuff. I notice the terrible camera work. I think Divine maybe looks the best in *Multiple Maniacs*, but I like them mostly because I know all the people and it's funny to me, like looking at old pictures of yourself. My really early films are so bad, but it's fun for people who know the actors to see what they looked like then. But if someone is having a festival of my stuff, I always tell them, "Make *Mondo Trasho* the hardest one to see, because if you've never seen any of my work and go see that first, you ain't coming back." (Laughs.) That's the one to see nowadays if you've seen all the other ones and want to see what it was like when it started. But to start on that film? Life's a little short.

IVES: When I was watching your films this time around, I watched *Desperate Living* first, then *Mondo Trasho*—and I actually watched *Mondo Trasho* again....

WATERS: Well, *Desperate Living* is certainly my least joyous movie. I must have been in a bad mood that year. But the real John Waters fanatics like that best. They always tell me that. I don't know why.

Edith Massey, an original Dreamlander, and Waters during the filming of Female Trouble.

Maybe because it's the most hidden-down-deep one.

IVES: It is down-deep. It's just unaesthetic.

WATERS: Although, Mortville has come true. [*Mortville is the central location for* Desperate Living, *a fictional town where criminals go to repent for their crimes.—JI*] There are Mortvilles now in every city, homeless little Mortvilles.

IVES: I guess I find *Mondo Trasho* the most poignant.

WATERS: Well, it is to me because so many of the people are dead now. That makes it poignant. Seeing Divine when he jumps out of that Cadillac in that gold outfit...

IVES: ...with his pants falling down...

WATERS: ...yes, because I was too cheap to mend the elastic, so through the whole movie his pants were falling down. And he handled it well. (Laughs.)

IVES: He had one hand on the back of his pants at all times.

WATERS: Well, they were hip-huggers without the elastic; it was a tough thing to pull off. So that to me is poignant, because that's a very Divine moment and that's gone. That's gone as youth, it's gone because he's dead, it's everything. When I see it, it's sad in a way, but it's happy because at least it's there. They had a tribute to Divine at the Castro Theater in San Francisco; they showed clips from all the movies, and that one got a very big reaction because many people remember the first time they ever saw Divine, and that was it. They go, "What the fuck is that?" Now they know who the fuck that was, but the first time they saw it they weren't quite sure. (Laughs.) And these are people who were fairly unshockable. That's who I made that movie for, people who thought they had seen every-

We were trying to do what the Manson family did, only with a movie camera.

thing.... In fan letters, people always say to me, "What *were* you? What could you have been like that you filmed this scene with eating shit?" The most shocking thing was that it was no big deal. (Laughs.) It was sort of a big deal that night after it was shot. Everybody said, "Do you believe that just happened?" It was surreal, and we knew that it was a moment of absurdity. It was pot humor, if only because I was on pot when I thought it up. The main characters in *Multiple Maniacs* [Waters, Divine, Mona Montgomery, Mink Stole, Mary Vivian Pearce, David Lochary] became an extended family, took LSD together and made those movies. We were trying to do what the Manson family did, only with a movie camera.... And you can see that rage, which was very anti-hippie. It was punk before it's time. It was that attitude of defiance, which there wasn't really a lot of then.

IVES: There was, but it came out in different ways.

WATERS: There was a war. And there was a war at home too. But you've got to remember that violence was the one taboo. Everything was "peace and love." Whatever you did, you didn't commit violence. Those people always got on my nerves, even though I wasn't violent, ever.

IVES: But towards the end of the sixties that was going away.

WATERS: It became Altamont versus Woodstock. I went to plenty of those riots.

IVES: Me, too.

WATERS: But I went because everybody looked good.... I thought it'd be a good chance to get a date. I mean, people look fairly good in a riot. It's a good look. Terrorists look good, too. Those scarves and the things over their eyes...it's a good look.

IVES: That's why terrorist movies are so great.

WATERS: Yeah. The woman who blew up [Rajiv] Gandhi. I'm not at all for what she did, but I loved that picture of her kneeling at his feet with that look of bliss on her face right before she blew herself up. To me there's something very appealing about that. I couldn't imagine doing what she did, but that's why I'm fascinated by it. If I could understand, I wouldn't be interested.

IVES: Back in the sixties, there was a paranoia that came partly from the drugs themselves and partly from the fact that because people were taking drugs, they were afraid of getting stopped by police. There was also the running through the streets and breaking things, or demonstrating, and the construction workers running around with crescent wrenches...

WATERS: ...who have long hair today.

IVES: Yeah, right, and earrings.

WATERS: The same people who would have beaten you up then have long hair now. Twenty, thirty years it took—but they're now dressing exactly the same as we were.

IVES: Now they beat you up because your hair's short.

WATERS: I had that in *Polyester*, the line: "Why don't you let that hair grow, boy? You look like some sort of fruit." It got a big laugh then because it was usually the other way around.

IVES: Is that paranoia part of what all that violence came from?

WATERS: I don't remember being paranoid. I remember some, like when a cop would stop you and you had long hair and everything, but I don't remember being especially paranoid. I remember thinking nothing bad could happen to us. We were so young, you know, we were invincible. But I don't remember being worried about being arrested—and I was arrested a couple of times. The day we were arrested for

I was as offended by the restrictions of hippie society as I was by the ones of the society I had just run from.

Mondo Trasho, they busted the nude guy one day and then they came back the next day and busted us all for obscenity. When they came to my house, I had a huge hunk of gold hash in my pocket and I talked the cops into, "Can I go up to my room and just get one thing?" Luckily they said yes, and I ditched the thing. Otherwise, that would have made it really worse, like...

IVES: ...Drug fiend.

WATERS: Right. But I remember being as offended by the constrictions of hippie society as I was by the ones in the society I had just run from, and that's what caused those movies. Back then, I lived in San Francisco for awhile and there were people who led communes who sort of said, "Okay, you can't eat meat." And they'd go around and tell other communes they shouldn't eat meat. So we did a raid on one of them and threw white sugar all over the floor. That was a very *Pink Flamingo*ish thing to do. It was joke terrorism.

IVES: Taking aim at different establishment characters?

WATERS: Yeah, but it was more aimed at the holier-than-thou peace movement creeps.

IVES: You've said that you were very angry. What were you angry about?

WATERS: Probably at society—the one that I ran from—and Catholics and school. But then I got into the bohemian world. I wish I had quit school when I was sixteen. I would have made probably one more movie. I just wasted those years. When the beatnik movement came out, it was the most fun of all, because it was the first thing that I could want to be. But it wasn't that big a thing then. When the hippie thing happened, it spread, and it sort of got too big for me. It was like having a book that you love and suddenly everyone loves it—it's not quite as good anymore. And I saw that

Waters and Iggy Pop (right) realized each other were both 1Y when the Gulf War broke out. According to Waters, that "basically means after hairdressers they'll take us."

the hippie movement had the same rules as the society I ran from, and I rebelled against that. I was into the whole Abbie Hoffman thing, completely. I used to go to different riots in different cities. I would go to Yale and set fires just for the fun of it. And, yes, I was against the Vietnam war, but I went right down [to the draft board] and got out of it. It wasn't some big trauma to me. I knew I was never going to go there. I just checked about five boxes [on the form] and they sent me home. It was easy.

IVES: It got harder, though.

WATERS: Yeah, but not when I was there. I checked bed-wetter, gay, junkie, every little silly thing. They didn't even make me take a physical. I had to go to the shrink there, but he just said, "What do you like to do in bed?" He was so perverted! He was easy to get through. I was there for two hours. And at the end of all that, I was one pound too thin. You had to be a hundred and thirty and I weighed a hundred and twenty-nine. I didn't even know about that, but I was classified "1Y." I remember when the Gulf War broke out, Iggy Pop and I said, "God, we're 1Y, do you think they'll call us?" (Laughs.) We both had the same classification, which basically means after hairdressers they'll take us. They never called me. (Laughs.) But you were talking about anger.... I guess I had anger at that [society and the war]. When I was young, I went through a whole period, two years, when I hung around with only black people—which is very racist, when you think about it. But it was exciting to me, it was new to our crowd, a world we had never been in: black Baltimore. And we got in so much trouble. Black cops used to stop us and say, "You can't do this. This isn't Greenwich Village." And we went to the drive-in together. We got busted.

IVES: You got busted for being with black people?

WATERS: Well, for drinking, but you can bet that's what got the attention—black and white, and girls and boys, all together.

IVES: Segregation wasn't on the books here, then, was it?

WATERS: No, I guess not. But that's when Wallace was running [in the presidential primary] here, and we used to go to those marches and picket, you know? It was scary, then. That whole H. Rap "Die, Nigger, Die" Brown thing happened in Cambridge, Maryland. Wallace was a big presence in political things here. And Agnew was the governor. So I went through that period, like they did in *Hairspray*. I used to hang around in this black record shop, and I got beat up for having a black girl as a date at a downtown dance. And I used to go to the Royal Theater to see James Brown. The Royal Theater was just like the Apollo in New York. And I'd get beat up, but it was worth it.

IVES: You'd get beat up by whites or blacks?

WATERS: I was the only white person there. When the concert let out, there was always a riot. At the time I went [to the Royal], the riots here in Baltimore were really amazing, I mean, whole neighborhoods are gone. The city was on fire. There was a tank out in front of my house, on Twenty-fifth Street.

> *I used to hang around in this black record shop, and I got beat up for having a black girl as a date.*

IVES: Did you live in a black neighborhood?

WATERS: Yeah, I lived in black neighborhoods my whole life after I moved away from my parents, until I moved to this house. At first I felt weird seeing white people walk by. I'm not used to it. But our days of hanging around with all black people were in high school. And by then Bonnie was forbidden to see me, so what would happen is we would get a fake date for her who would go pick her up, and I'd wait on the corner.... Only sometimes we couldn't get fake dates, so she'd get real ones and jump out of the car.

IVES: Your parents didn't object, or punish you, for all this stuff?

WATERS: They didn't know about a lot of it. They were very uptight about it, but they indulged me. They never told me to get out. They would deny this, but they didn't like me hanging out with black friends. They would never come out and say something that racist, but it was an unspoken thing. Most suburban white parents, it was just foreign to them. But being a beatnik, you *had* to have integrated friends, and go to jazz clubs, and yell out, "All right!" for no apparent reason. That was part of being a beatnik. But then it got even more confusing because some of us were gay. Girls were always so confused. They never could quite get what was going on. And the crowd of people I hang around with is still like that. I have many heterosexual men friends in Baltimore who are fag hags, and they're not closet queens. That's a Baltimore phenomenon.

IVES: Provincetown, too. I suppose in a sense that was what I was.

WATERS: (Laughs.) Right. But that's rare. I won't name names, but some of the people we hang around with are still like that. And it confuses people.

IVES: Pat [Moran] is straight. She's married, and has kids, and leads her version of a normal life.

WATERS: But in Pat's mind, gay men liberated her, got her out of suburbia. Before I met her, you know, she was a raging fag hag. And she is forever loyal to fag-hagism, because they rescued her from a boring life. So our friends were always completely mixed, sexually. It was so mixed that the parents were uptight, and then when we threw in black friends on top of it all, they didn't know what to do about it. And not only that, it was also all classes. There were some rich kids and some hillbillies.... The group of people we hung around with was so mixed; every person was from a completely different background. We had a gang mentality, in a way. We traveled in packs.

IVES: But you don't do that anymore?

WATERS: I still feel a certain gangmanship with the ones who are still alive.

IVES: But, in terms of where you get your stories—do you build them around the characters in your life?

WATERS: Well, I don't know. I certainly use stories that people tell me— a certain humor still that comes from that—and I still see a lot of people. I've been friends with a lot of my friends for twenty-five years, and it's certainly a good feeling. I'm still in touch with the people from those days, but it's different now. I mean, we haven't been to any riots this week. Not that I wouldn't—I'd go to an AIDS riot. I'm surprised that hasn't happened, to be honest with you. I think it will in the nineties. I think there'll be gay terrorism soon.

IVES: What is the relationship, in terms of the stories that you've written, between gangs and family?

WATERS: It's the same. A gang is an attempt at making the family situation better. I think the best gang members are fleeing from something.

IVES: Are they fleeing from family?

WATERS: In many cases, yeah. I'm not saying I did—I like my family. But a gang is an extended family. I think its good, because eventually your parents die before your gang does. To be in a gang—especially a gang whose colors are humor—has always been very satisfying to me. Those people who are card-carrying Dreamland members are my closest friends. [*Dreamland Studios is what Waters called his first apartment, and all his early films credited Dreamland Studios as the production company. All original members of the Waters troupe are referred to as Dreamlanders.—JI*] They've been through many, many thick and thin parts of my life. Most people haven't had friends for that long.

IVES: The gangs in your films are different—on the surface—from an actual street gang, in the sense that you're talking about a group of friends who go through a lot of things together.

WATERS: But in the gangs in the movies there is still that loyalty, that sense of style and humor that has defined them, and the fact that the gang is based on what society is against. They're always the heroes in my movies.

IVES: You seem to be exploring damaged families a lot in your films.

WATERS: Well, there's always a war between two groups of damaged families, but the families who are at peace with their damage are the heroes—and have turned their damage into a style.

IVES: There's a lot of damage in *Female Trouble*, isn't there?

WATERS: But it has a happy ending because she died famous, which is all she cared about. So the electric chair is a very happy ending.

IVES: Isn't that the film with the Christmas tree falling? She throws her mother under the Christmas tree and runs out. That's a pretty damaged family relationship.

WATERS: Yeah. But also, of all my movies, that is one of the most famous scenes that gets the laughs. Everybody has some damage in their family, but nobody acts that horrible with their mother. That's why everyone laughed; they can remember fights they had with their parents, but no one knocks a Christmas tree over on their mother.

IVES: Right. And then she ran out...

WATERS: ...screaming, "Fuck you! I hate! You're not my parents! You awful people. (Laughs.)

IVES: But is that a theme?

WATERS: I guess it is, though I don't think of it that way. I think of *Female Trouble* as Dawn Davenport just trying to get through her life, and so many bad things happen to her. People are jealous of her style and take her over and use her. But that's because she's really better than any of them. It's the same way in *Pink Flamingos*—the Marbles are actually filthier than Divine. [*Connie and Raymond Marble, played by Mink Stole and David Lochary, were the chief antagonists in* Pink Flamingos.—JI]

IVES: What is filthiness?

WATERS: Well, in that movie, filthiness was punk. There was no name for it then, but filthiness was exactly what punk meant when it started.

IVES: It strikes me that some of your heroes talk about doing evil, nasty things but, really, they care about people. They rescue orphans. The other people are stealing children and abusing children and things that are more normally thought of as evil.

WATERS: And *are* evil. But even though our society thinks of what my heroes are doing as evil, it's really basically harmless. Eating shit doesn't hurt anyone.

IVES: Well, in *Multiple Maniacs*, they did kill a few people.

WATERS: Oh, yeah.

IVES: For fun.

WATERS: But those were people who paid money to come gawk at their neuroses. Liberals. (Laughs.)

IVES: Do you ever think about the themes—apart from the humor—in your films?

WATERS: No. Only when I talk to journalists or read things that have been written. A lot of times I read things and think, "Oh, that's probably true. I never thought of it."

IVES: Most of your writings don't really discuss the themes.

WATERS: No, not much. There are a couple of books, like *Midnight Movies* [by J. Hoberman], that are so intricate that I think, "This is really funny, because I never thought of this before in my life." It's not that they're wrong; I mean, I went to a shrink, and he always used to laugh and say we could do a book together: *A Shrink Analyzes Your Movies*. Talk about exploitation.

IVES: That'd make a great TV show.

WATERS: I know. For a psychiatrist, they're probably perfect to analyze.

IVES: But doesn't that mean that some of that stuff *is* in there?

WATERS: Sure. It's in *me* some-where. But maybe how I feel about it isn't exactly like that. I don't live the life of the charac-

> *Underdogs who win are the ultimate heroes.*

ters, but I can imagine it. And certainly there are things that are repeated, themes that always come up.

IVES: What are they?

WATERS: That underdogs who win are the ultimate heroes and—I've said this a million times, but it's true—I respect people who exaggerate disadvantages and turn them into a style.

IVES: What about the theme of the tormented woman? Why is that in there?

Divine was "led to spiritual enlightenment by the Infant of Prague" in Multiple Maniacs.

WATERS: Because Divine played it so well. Because I make better girl movies than boy movies. *Cry-Baby* was the only boy movie I ever made, and a lot of people didn't like it as much. Maybe that's why. I don't know why.

IVES: It seems to me there's a lot of that [tormented women], though, starting with *Mondo Trasho.*

WATERS: She does have a bad day.

IVES: Well, they both do. Divine has a bad day, but Bonnie has a...

WATERS: ...she has a really bad day. She gets "shrimped" and run over by a car. Certainly not a good way to spend a Sunday.

IVES: And then she ends up in the snake pit.

WATERS: Yeah, but then she gets magic feet, you see. So she meets somebody who alters her style, and those magic feet bring her happiness and take her to all different places. [*See Timeline for full synopsis and commentary.*—*JI*] But at the end she's still getting harassed by people making rude comments.

IVES: I thought it was a sad ending.

WATERS: Yeah, I guess now that I think about it, it kind of is, except she should have risen above that when they were gossiping about her. She should have put a pair of heels on those feet. You know? And walked happily on. Which is what it was about.

IVES: But the feet were also a tragedy, weren't they?

WATERS: Not to me.

IVES: She had nice feet and then she had ugly feet.

WATERS: Well, they weren't ugly to me. To me they were surreal feet. All they were, were dollar-ninety-eight monster feet from a joke shop.

IVES: They looked like they'd been soaked for a few weeks.

WATERS: I don't think they had. Well, she walked through pig shit. Maybe we filmed that first and had to sterilize them. (Laughs.) I don't remember. But to me the feet were happy, in a way. The feet gave her magic powers.

IVES: They only gave her the power to escape from one bad scene to another.

WATERS: Well, she lived.

IVES: That's true; it did bring her back to life.

WATERS: And she had to deal with people making fun of her.

IVES: What about Divine's character in *Polyester?* She's horribly tormented.

WATERS: Yes, she is, but in a way that everybody finds funny. There is a certain humor in everything going wrong one day in your life. "What's the worst thing that can happen to you?" can be funny, because it's not real. It wouldn't be funny in real life at all. It would be really sad, but in a movie theater, maybe it's so sad that it's funny. Nobody could have that bad a day. Everything goes wrong.

IVES: I just kept thinking of the Book of Job.

WATERS: I haven't read that in a while.

IVES: But you do have all these religious themes.

WATERS: Well, certainly, tormentedness is taught in the Catholic Church. You're taught that it makes you divine to—to use the word that they did use a lot—suffer. I mean, crucifying somebody, that's supposed to be nice? I don't get it. But that Catholic obsession with suffering has heavily colored my sense of humor. Maybe tormented women in my film are what we...we're taught to worship a tormented man. So, its not so odd.

IVES: Were you conscious of all these things?

WATERS: No, not at all. I never thought of that. Ever. I thought, "What would make me laugh?" And I still think of that.... But obviously I'm saying something, or I wouldn't go through all the trouble it is to make these movies. The healthiest thing I ever think of is that all you can do is laugh when things are bad. It's the only way to not cry. It's mentally healthy for me to turn everything into humor. And maybe it's protection, too.

IVES: Do you think of yourself as an artist?

WATERS: It's a word I'm very, very uncomfortable with. I'm very flattered if someone else calls me that, but I don't think it is up to me. It's up to the public to decide if you're an artist. It's up to history to decide if you're truly an artist. If your work survives you, for how long? That's how good of an artist you were. I cringe when I meet people and say, "What do you do?" and they say, "I'm an artist." I feel like telling them, "Says who?" So I don't use that term. I think I'm a humorist and a writer.

IVES: But in *Shock Value* you said—it seemed rather proudly—that you felt very good that your films have no redeeming social value.

WATERS: Maybe that was posturing in the other direction, looking back on it. There are certain lines in that book that I'll never live down—or up to. Like saying if someone vomits during my film it's like a standing ovation. I said that tongue-in-cheek, because people did vomit in my film but it was because they were drunk. They would have puked if it was *The Sound of Music*. But about having no redeeming social value...my films aren't meant to change anything, but if they ever did I'd be happy. I said before, "Maybe I've made trash one-millionth more respectable." And that sounds too close to bragging for me to be comfortable with it.

IVES: In terms of mass culture, don't you think the country has moved more towards you?

WATERS: Toward my sense of humor? Yes. But I don't know if that's because of me.

IVES: Has society become more willing to look at itself?

WATERS: To laugh at their bad points? Yes. To laugh at everything that's horrible, yes. Much, much more.

IVES: So what does that make you feel you ought to do? Does it make you want to change direction in any way?

WATERS: No. But if I did things that I used to do, if I did them now, it would be too obvious and would be trying too hard. You can't purposely make a cult movie. Those movies were fairly spontaneous at the time. They were not calculated to be anything. I mean, I knew what I was doing—I read *Variety* all the time, so I knew that you could make fun of an exploitation movie and that's what I was trying to do—but I didn't intellectualize it. And I certainly knew enough to anti-intellectualize it for the press.

IVES: Why are you tackling issues more openly in your movies now?

WATERS: Well, in *Hairspray* I did. Everybody thinks it's so safe now, but it was very touchy to make a movie that was a comedy about the civil rights movement. As a white man. It was really risky, because people really would get uptight. If I'd gone out and pitched that saying, "It's a comedy about civil rights," I don't know if they would have said yes.

IVES: Is that how you saw it when you wrote it?

WATERS: Yes, that was part of it, to make fun of a liberal's taboo. But, oddly enough, those people didn't rise to the bait. Maybe it wasn't the bait I thought it was. No one was ever offended by that. I don't think I got one review in the whole world that was offended by that. The sacred cow wasn't as strong as I thought, which is probably one of the reasons for its success.

IVES: You were further away from the civil rights movement by then, that's the difference.

WATERS: That's it. How brave was it to be a pro-civil rights movie in 1987? To say yes, I think blacks should be allowed to dance on television—it's not a real tough position to take. Although, in the South, there were people who said, "She kissed a what?" I had interracial kids kissing, which is still a taboo. Spike's certainly right in *Jungle Fever*, because that is still a major taboo.

IVES: Did you like that movie?

WATERS: Yes.

IVES: A lot?

WATERS: More than most. I even like all the stuff he says that gets on all white people's nerves, because he doesn't let up. Ever. And it is annoying sometimes, but I'm not black. If I were black, I'd be so *for* him. And I love it when he says things like, "You can't be racist if you're black." It makes people crazy when they read that stuff. (Laughs.)

IVES: Do you think you ever learn anything from reviews, criticism?

WATERS: It's politically incorrect for a director to say yes, but yes.

IVES: Politically incorrect?

WATERS: Directorially incorrect. But yes, I have. And I guess if they all say one thing, you have to at least pay some attention to it. Reviewers have mostly been very fair to me—even the ones who don't like it. The only times they weren't was in a few cases for *Cry-Baby*. The meanest reviews were from the people who championed me in the beginning when no one else would. They went into it not liking the fact that I made a movie for Universal, I think. But I can understand that. I might feel the same way. The funny thing to me—and I knew this would happen—was that the people who said they wished it [*Cry-Baby*] had been more like *Pink Flamingos*, hated *Pink Flamingos*. Very few liked it then, and I remember which ones did.

> *The only way I could do terrorism at this point in my career would be to make a Hollywood movie that would reach every person—and make them crazy.*

IVES: Would you ever go back to guerilla filmmaking?

WATERS: No.... It wouldn't work, because I'm forty-five, not twenty. Where's that rage? I'm not sleeping in my car, which I was then. I'm all for that when you're twenty. That's what I said in that *Newsweek* article—we've got to make it cool to be poor again. That's what kids have got to do. When we were growing up, it was cool to be poor. It was embarrassing to have money; if people did, they hid it. It isn't like that now, and that's a shame because the most un-American thing you can do is want to be poor. That really makes people nervous. That's terrorism at it's most. The only way I could do terrorism at my age—at this position in my career—would be to do a Hollywood movie that could reach every person and make them crazy.

IVES: How would you do that?

WATERS: I'm still trying, in my own way. If I made a movie now that was as raw as *Pink Flamingos*, where would you show it? They don't even have midnight movies anymore. It would be a video hit.

IVES: You'd have to put stars in it.

WATERS: You couldn't do it for ten thousand dollars. There's none of those taboos left. *Poison* and *Superstar* [*two recent films directed by Todd Haynes—JI*] are the first movies I've seen that remind me of the spirit of the old days. But there's so much hype now, so quickly.... Critics rush to *like* them instead of condemn them—that's the problem today. I wrote him [Todd Haynes] after he got this really mean review in the *Hollywood Reporter*, and I said, "I'm so jealous of that review." It was the perfect kind of review that would make you go see it, you know: "...outraged and appalled at this thing. Let's stop this right here, it's gone far enough!" That's the best kind of review, but you don't see many of them. Rex Reed always gave us those. He continues to; he said *Hairspray* was "gross." (Laughs.) Gross? How *could* he? I liked that. We all wait every year for his review to come, and we just roar when we read them. It's a tradition. He's the only one who still rises to the bait. And he rose every time.

IVES: Didn't you feel *Cry-Baby* was too easy for everybody? There wasn't enough conflict?

WATERS: I think it's a weirder movie than *Hairspray*. So did the rating board; the rating was more restricted [PG-13 rather than PG]. The difference was that it did not have Divine as a reference point, which there was nothing I could do about. The heroes were too normal for a John Waters movie. On opening night, when I walked into the Waverly Theater—which has always been sort of my home for my movies in New York—and there were two empty seats, I knew it was not going to work. They should have turned away a hundred people. I got back in the limo and I knew. I went to the hotel and went to bed, and the next day I knew exactly what the numbers were going to be. This was not good. But the weird thing was that *Cry-Baby* played in fifteen hundred theaters; *Hairspray* only played in two hundred and something. *Cry-Baby* played in all

the theaters I had never played in. It didn't do well in those theaters, but *Hairspray* never even played in them.

IVES: So it's an accomplishment to get into those theaters?

WATERS: Yes. And in those towns—little one-movie-theater towns—
they thought it was as weird, believe me this is hard to imagine, as
Pink Flamingos. They were totally baffled by it. So I tried to learn
why they didn't like it. They really didn't get it. That's why I'm glad
to do a contemporary movie this time. That's what I learned: I've
done every generation that I've ever been alive in, and it's time to get
back to the present. I'm through with doing period movies.

IVES: What about the gimmicks, like...

WATERS: ...Odorama [from *Polyester*]?

IVES: ...like flying through the air in *Cry-Baby?*

WATERS: I still like it. Audiences don't. It's surrealism in the middle of
a movie that's supposed to be realistic. I have no problem with that;
audiences do. You don't fly off of a motorcycle through the air and
land in someone's arms, in real life.

IVES: It's a Hollywoody kind of thing to do, in a sense.

WATERS: It's a joke of a romantic ending; it's such a cliche. But if you
don't know the cliche, the joke doesn't work. I may be wrong, but I
think that's basically what they didn't like. Sixteen-year-old kids really didn't go for that. I never had to worry about them before. I want
to make an R-rated movie—then they can't come.... Those problems
were not in Europe at all.

IVES: Well, it probably also had to do with...

WATERS: ...with Universal.... United International Pictures is one of the
strongest ones [internationally]. I loved all that. Having that mus-
cle behind me. Just to see the billboards! I never thought I would
ever see the day when I would see Hollywood billboards for one of
my films. The biggest high of *Cry-Baby* was that it was an official
selection at the Cannes Film Festival. The midnight screening was
completely sold out. Standing ovation. They loved it. Standing at
the top of that red carpet and turning around with eight million pap-
parazzi, with Pat and Ricki Lake and Rachel [Talalay], my producer, it was a huge high to me. That was a fantasy that I wanted since
I was fourteen. So *Cry-Baby* was a good experience for me in the long
run. Out of all my movies, it was probably the happiest on the set.
There were some problems, but I think people had a lot of fun working on it. Nobody hated each other when it was over, or anything.

AT LAST. . . . A "GUTTER FILM"

**JOHN
WATERS'**

MONDO TRASHO

WORLD PREMERE march 14,15,16-baltimore, md.-9 shows, 140 seats 1225 admissions

★ beaux arts-tampa, fla.- april 11th, 12th   4 shows

★ santa barbara museum of art-june 13,14   3 shows

★ cinema kenmore square, boston- july 25, 26 2 shows

★ art cinema, provincetown- aug 19   s.r.o.   200 turned away

★ u-p screen, n.y.c.- sept. 5,6   4 shows

★ bard college, n.y.- sept. 30 1 show

**"an underground epic of all
that is trashy in life"** PROVINCETOWN
ADVOCATE

Original trade advertisement sent out by Waters in 1969.

IVES: Did you ever have that problem with your early movies?

WATERS: No. I didn't. But *Hairspray* had the best party in the middle of it—it was almost magical. The wrap parties at the end are always awful; everybody is so tired and gross. But every movie has a spontaneous party right about in the middle of shooting. When I look back on it, the party in *Hairspray* should have been a good sign that movie was going to win. It was on the art director's pier and it was a beautiful night. All of the kids were doing the dances—it was really one of those nights that you remember. Sometimes those nights can predict, "That's the mood of the film." And sometimes when all those kids were dancing [on screen], that mood was transferred inside the theater. When people saw that, they liked it.... You'd be surprised. On the *Hairspray* test, when we first did it, all of the white teen-age boys said they hated it. They refused to admit they could root for a fat girl. They walked out. Then when it opened, the exit polls came out that they liked it best—which just goes to show you. All that money and they give you conflicting reports....

IVES: Do you have any undeveloped projects sitting in the back of your mind?

WATERS: I never do. I never think about it, either. When it's time for me to go work, then I go in there and I think about it. I mean, I work. When I'm in the middle of writing a project, I certainly dream about it. Things remind me all the time. I have little notes I write in my book, like those bad Woody Allen director characters in his films. (Laughs.) I don't have a tape recorder, but I do have little pads. I'm thinking about it all the time because I'm so into it, living the whole thing. I mean, you wake up and that's what you think about.

IVES: The only one you never did was *Flamingos Forever?*

WATERS: Right. But that became a book, so now I could never do it.

IVES: You couldn't do that without Divine?

WATERS: Or Edie [Massey], either. It just wouldn't work. It'd be a substitute cast—that's terrible.

IVES: Were Cotton and Crackers meant to be the same actors also?

WATERS: Yes.

IVES: Why did you call the characters Cotton 2 and Crackers 2 in the script?

WATERS: In case we couldn't get them. I knew Bonnie [Mary Vivian Pearce] was willing but Danny [Mills] probably wouldn't have done it. He would never do another one with me after *Pink Flamingos*....

IVES: *Pink Flamingos* had a good effect on some of the actors' careers.

WATERS: Oh, yeah. It gave everybody some kind of visibility that they didn't have before. All the old movies had never even played in New York. But you know what really gave Divine all the opportunities? *Hairspray*, in a week. In *Pink Flamingos*, everybody knew Divine but they were terrified of him. He had to battle that his whole life—people thinking he was really like that. In real life he was so *unlike* that. His humor could be like that, but he himself was hardly like that.

IVES: He was very gentle.

WATERS: Yes, very quiet. But...people were so terrified of him, what role could he get? That was his problem. He was so closely identified with that role that it was difficult for him to get work. That's why he did the rock star thing; it was a way to work, to pay the bills. But I think after *Hairspray* he would have...I know he already had offers from that before he died. That was the break he was looking for, not *Pink Flamingos*. *Pink Flamingos* gave him incredible notoriety, which is sometimes very, very hard for an actor. To ever live down the shit-eating. At the end, he joked about it with me, but underneath it all he was very wary about it, because twenty years later that was still the first question they always asked him.

IVES: But I think he was a great actor.

WATERS: I think he was too. And he got good reviews.

IVES: How much of that came from you?

WATERS: I think he was comfortable with me and he knew how to say the lines right. He could just talk; I didn't have to direct him at the end. But Divine was great at taking direction; I think he felt more confident if the director told him exactly what he wanted rather than just going out there and ad libbing. I think what made Divine the most nervous were directors who were intimidated by him. And Divine, in real life, was the opposite of intimidating. He was gentle, and he looked kind of peculiar—he looked almost like a holy man. (Laughs.) Not like what people think. He looked like some sort of mad religious figure. He could be very, very funny.

IVES: But he was a lot quieter than most of the other people.

WATERS: And he was shy around strangers. Even with the press, he was almost reserved about what he was. He was nervous about it. He was scared of them, basically, because they'd come in with this one idea of what he was going to be like and that's what they'd write, no matter what he said.

IVES: Right, but the role in *Hairspray* was so different.

WATERS: That's why he finally got really good offers. I mean, he started his career playing a homicidal maniac and ended playing a loving mother—if that's not good acting, what is? Especially when you're a man. (Laughs.) That was the thing that we always tried to give an audience: a Divine image that was different. In *Polyester* he played like a polyester housewife, completely different from the chainsaw type he almost was in *Pink Flamingos*. Mad Maxina or something.

> *Divine started his career playing a homicidal maniac and ended up playing a loving mother. If that's not good acting, what is?*

IVES: Did you invent his name?

WATERS: Yep. And it didn't come from the Genet book like everybody thinks, although that might have had a subconscious influence that I don't remember. I read *Our Lady of the Flowers* and loved it. But Divine came from Catholicism because it was a word they used a lot. I gave it to him in *Roman Candles*, which was influenced by the Warhol films and that kind of anger. People had those kind of names in all of those underground films.

IVES: Glenn didn't make it?

WATERS: Yeah. It just didn't. And when he became Divine professionally, he became another person. He wasn't Glenn. Underneath it all, alone, he wasn't Glenn. He always wanted to not be Glenn. Glenn didn't leave his house until he was seventeen years old. He would admit he was a nerd in high school—with Gina Lollobrigida lurking inside.

IVES: It's hard thinking about some of these people now that they're dead....

WATERS: It's very hard, but one good thing is that he never knew. He went to sleep and never woke up. He never, ever knew.

IVES: What filmmakers are your major influences?

WATERS: Walt Disney, *The Wizard of Oz*, William Castle, Russ Meyer, Bergman, Fellini, Warhol, the Kuchar Brothers , and Fassbinder. I've probably forgotten some.

IVES: Bunuel?

WATERS: Yes, Bunuel.

IVES: Polanski? Early Polanski?

WATERS: Polanski's so weird because of what happened. I mean with the murders. [*Polanski's wife, Sharon Tate, was murdered by the Manson "family."* —*JI*] But yes, I like Polanski's films very much. Especially

The Tenant and *Repulsion*.

IVES: And *Cul-de-Sac*.

WATERS: Yes. I loved *Cul-de-Sac*. I've had the poster for that for years.

IVES: What about Edgar Ulmer? Did you ever see *Detour*?

WATERS: Yes, maybe I saw *Detour*, but what else did he make? I haven't seen many of them. I really didn't see all those *noir*-type films when I was growing up. If I've seen any of them, it has been later in my life—way later.

IVES: *Gun Crazy*?

WATERS: Yeah, I like that. I liked Samuel Fuller a lot. *The Naked Kiss* was a big influence on me, but he hates that movie. When I brought it up to him, he started screaming at me.

IVES: And Nick Ray's early films?

WATERS: Let's say I didn't see them when I was young, so they weren't an influence. I've only seen them later in life, when I look at them in a studied way. I never went on a weekend and saw them playing somewhere, which is how you should have seen them—to be an influence on you. I saw them later in life because I'd read about them so much, which is very different. I don't know if they influence you then. I think what influences you is movies that you innocently see that make you crazy in a wonderful way. Or even discover on your own.

IVES: You didn't really start out thinking you were going to be a filmmaker.

WATERS: No, I didn't. I wanted to be that as soon as I knew about underground film, and that movement started in the sixties.... I think sixteen is fairly early to know what you want to do. I believed the films would work. None of the people I worked with ever took it seriously, in the beginning.

> *The drive-in was my temple. I went every night.*

IVES: But from the very beginning you set out...

WATERS: I was too *fifteen* to think of being older. I thought I wouldn't be older. I thought I'd probably die at a young age.

IVES: You don't realize you're fated to turn out like your parents.

WATERS: Oh, no, you never realize that.

IVES: My stepfather got me into movies. We used to sit up every night, watching *The Late Show*. He used to call them "Italian boobie flicks."

WATERS: The drive-in was my temple. I literally went to the drive-in

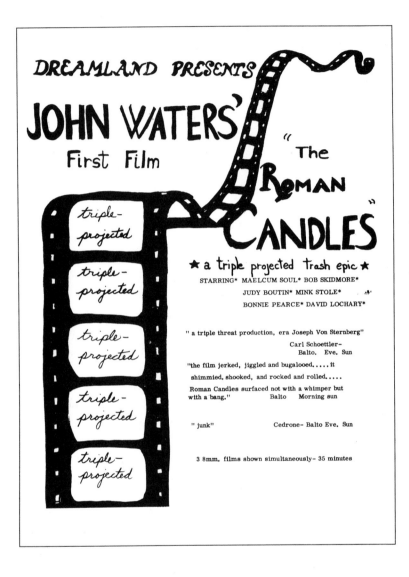

Original trade advertisement sent out by Waters in 1965.

every night, because it was the only place where you could go unsu-
pervised. And we would drink beer and smoke pot and do other stuff.

IVES: But that was only in the summer.

WATERS: No. We went in the dead of winter too. I've been to the drive-in in the snow. It was great. They really had to play exploitation stuff, because no one would go otherwise. That's when I saw the most hideous of them all. And you'd have those heaters that you put in the car, and they'd catch your car on fire. Flames would shoot up.... Those drive-in years are where my film knowledge came from, in one direction—all the exploitation movies. I saw all those movies many, many times; we'd go every night of the week. But then I would go to New York and see all the underground movies, and the Bergman movies at the college. Bergman is everything I like, subject matter-wise. Despair. It was a high. (Laughs.) All of those influences were different, but they were all about extreme kinds of moods.

IVES: What about old Hollywood, Bette Davis, James Cagney, and all that stuff?

WATERS: I never liked that kind of film classic.... Bette Davis was an influence on me when she did *Whatever Happened to Baby Jane?* And the eye patch, whatever that one was called [*The Anniversary*]. That's my kind of Bette Davis movie.... Douglas Sirk was a big influence. I still love his melodramas, you know, what they called "women's pictures," what they always said was sort of dime-store glamour.

IVES: Did he do *Imitation of Life?*

WATERS: Yes. And *Written on the Wind.* I liked all of them. *Boom [An Elizabeth Taylor, Richard Burton vehicle released in 1968—JI]* is my all-time, favorite bad Hollywood movie. I don't know that any movie could effect me today like that one did then. I still love bad movies, but it's not the same.

IVES: What do you see now?

WATERS: Not everything.... The last movie I really liked was *Angel at My Table*—Jane Campion—but it's hardly a commercial Hollywood movie. The last commercial Hollywood movie I liked was probably *Jungle Fever.*

IVES: And it's not really a big Hollywood movie. It was made by a studio, but...

WATERS: ...but that's what I mean. That's becoming what a Hollywood movie is today—which is good.

IVES: Did you see *Teen-age Mutant Ninja Turtles?*

WATERS: Yes. But I also saw *Milo and Otis.* Alone in the Beverly Center [in West Hollywood]. And families moved from me, and pulled their kids away, because I went and saw a matinee alone. I guess it did look weird. When I bought the ticket, the woman gave me a child molester look. And I sat there, and I saw people move—just because there was no other single male adult watching *Milo and Otis* in a matinee.

IVES: You should have worn a raincoat.

WATERS: No. The same thing happened at the *Care Bears* movie I went to see.

IVES: Do you like animated movies?

WATERS: No. I went to see *Milo and Otis* because it isn't animated, and it was Japanese, and I thought maybe they had done this incredible movie with this cat and dog while kids yelled. But it wasn't that incredible. And I had to sit there saying, "Awwww...."

IVES: Did you see *The Little Mermaid?*

WATERS: It had Divine in it. Divine would have wanted money from Disney. (Laughs.) I don't know how everybody said Divine would have loved it. Well, dead he would have loved it. I don't know if he would have loved it alive.

IVES: What about Warhol? We've mentioned him briefly, but...did you like his stuff?

WATERS: Yes, very much. He was a new kind of cool in the sixties— hip, gay, people on drugs. No one had done that before him. No one had said the word "fag hag" in a movie before. He broke a lot of barriers in a very hip, New York way that was certainly an influence on me. I love *Chelsea Girls.* I think it's a great movie. And I liked all the Paul Morrissey films, too. Remember the Andy Warhol Garrett Theater? He's the only director that I know who's had a whole theater named after him for a while....

IVES: The Orson Welles in Boston.

WATERS: ...That's when there were still taboos.

IVES: And you wanted to break them?

WATERS: Well, I wanted to have fun with them. I wanted to laugh about breaking them.

IVES: I think Andy's work had a lot less substance, as a rule, than yours.

WATERS: But he had a lot of style. He did bad first, and I don't mean the movie *Bad.* He purposely baited people.

IVES: He did *Trash*.

WATERS: He did the Empire State one. He never even saw that movie; no one ever saw that movie completely. That film was twelve hours, it was the same shot. The sleeping thing was not continuous. So he used that for publicity; that was terrorism, and people responded to it like that. The same thing with putting a soup can on the wall. He did it first—way first—and it changed everything. And then all the abstract expressionists were like the Motown girls when the Beatles came out: a whole art movement was finished—overnight.

IVES: What's your feeling about sex in films?

WATERS: In all my films, sex is made to look ludicrous. I like sex. Although, in a way it can never be that great because I didn't think it up. I resent instinct.

IVES: Instinct?

WATERS: Yes, in the same way that I resent that we have to go to the bathroom and eat—I don't have any choice in that matter. Anything that we have to do can never be that great. If I thought, "Hey, let's do this," and no one had ever done it before, it would really be fun. But I have no choice other than to think this stuff up in my mind, you know? That's the only down to sex—I didn't think it up. I want to know who thought it up. And it is ludicrous. No matter what your preference, you can always say, "Well, there sure are a lot of ludicrous positions." (Laughs.) That's what I try to put in the movie, that kind of ludicrousness. In the long run, people's sexuality makes very little difference. No matter what you do in bed, everybody is fairly the same emotionally. That's the most interesting part of it, and that's what makes people the most crazy about it.

IVES: *Pink Flamingos* probably had the most sex in it.

WATERS: But it was fake sex. Danny didn't even get a real hard-on. He had a Hollywood loaf. (Laughs.) People said it was hard-core, but I said, "Well, sort of." The sex in that film was all...

IVES: ...it was phony hard-core.

WATERS: Yes. It was funny hard-core, with people doing ludicrous monologues while they're having sex. That's not real sex. The ugliest sex scene I ever did was Divine fucking himself [in *Female Trouble*]. It's rather unjoyous on a filthy mattress in a dump. (Laughs.) I remember filming that. The garbage men were there just, like, looking...and then they were more shocked when we came back two hours later with Divine in a complete other outfit dressed as a woman. [*Divine played both members of the couple.—JI*] So sex is like everything in the movie—it's another sick joke. In real life it can be and it can't be. But what fascinates me about sex is that it is this instinct and that we basically have no choice about it. That diminishes its glamour.

> *Sex is like everything else in my movies; it's another sick joke.*

IVES: You moved away from gore.

WATERS: Yes, because it was over with. Hollywood did gore. They still do. There's no punch left in gore.

IVES: And now you've kind of moved away from sex?

WATERS: When I had in my contract that I was doing a PG movie, what was the point of filming a sex scene? I'd have to cut it out.... If Ricki Lake had fucked everybody in the show in the middle of *Hairspray,* I don't think audiences would have gone for it. I don't think it would have been in the spirit of that film. But I'm not through with sex scenes. I think they are the most difficult. Everyone is the most uncomfortable on those scenes with kissing and everything—including the actors. It's an intimate thing you have to like fake. But it's also real in some ways, because when you kiss somebody, you have to physically do it.... But I always try to make my sex scenes funny, too. I want the actors to not be embarrassed. If they're going to do any nudity, I want them to look great. Unless they're supposed to look hideous, which in my movies means great, anyway.

IVES: Did you have any problems with that in your earlier films? Were the actors ever uptight?

WATERS: I think Divine and Danny both were. They knew each other and they were friends, so it was a little embarrassing, [*The fellatio scene in* Pink Flamingos—*JI*] but that was pre-AIDS. Don't forget, things were so different then. It's really hard to imagine even doing that scene today. And it's the one scene I do regret from *Pink Flamingos.* If I had my way, it would be cut out. But I can't do that, because people would think the film was censored.

IVES: Why would you cut it out?

WATERS: For Divine's dignity. *Pink Flamingos* came out the same year as *Deep Throat,* when porno-chic was at it's peak. I put that scene in as a joke on that. But that joke has been lost today. People don't understand it, so it makes them uncomfortable to watch it. It makes me uncomfortable, to be honest with you.

IVES: There are European directors who still use it all the time. Bellocchio...

WATERS: Yeah. I would never have real sex in a movie, but in *Cry-Baby* I had that incredible French-kissing thing. I'm surprised no one objected to doing that. That is certainly in the tradition of a John Waters sex scene. It was one of the biggest laughs in the whole movie. The studio never wanted me to cut that out because in every test it got the second-biggest laugh. The first-biggest was when Hatchet- Face jumped through the movie screen in the 3-D scene.... So I'm not through with sex, but I never even think about doing gore anymore.

IVES: But you don't need to do gore anymore because you're not trying to shock in the same way. You're doing it more subtly in a sense.

WATERS: Yeah, but I was trying to shock you a little in the French-kissing scene in *Cry-Baby*. People want a couple of shots like that when they come into my movies, you know? They're reference points. One critic said that, and it's true. It's almost like it's comforting.

IVES: Are your films gay films in some way?

WATERS: No. Well, yes and no. Yes, if you listed around six other adjectives along with the word "gay."

IVES: What six adjectives?

WATERS: I'm not denying that gay sensibilities are in there, but I think black humor—not meaning racially—is first. Gay humor is a little part of that, but I've seen *Pink Flamingos* get the same reaction from bikers and drag queens. I've seen it with mental patients. I've seen it with prisoners. I've seen it with middle-class college students. And the ones who like it, all like it for the same reason—because it's funny. I'm glad that I became known a while ago, so I didn't have to deal with the question of whether I am first a gay filmmaker. That puts you in a corner. Being gay certainly led to the humor in my movies; it's part of me, so it's part of what I think is funny. But I don't think that being gay makes you good or bad. There are gay directors who are terrible. I don't think it makes that much difference. All of the people who have been with me from the beginning are very evenly divided along sexual lines. Many of them are straight; it's completely mixed and always has been. That's what I've always like best— being friends with a completely mixed bunch of people. It's much more interesting when they talk about their personal lives.

IVES: But in the early days in Provincetown—no matter who you were sleeping with or what you were doing—there was a gay-influenced society. And it wasn't just in Provincetown. It was in New York, San Francisco, Los Angeles.

WATERS: Gay-influenced? Art *always* was. What do you think Noel Coward was talking about? It's just that before gay liberation, nobody said it. Everybody knew it; they just didn't talk about it. Show business has always had a lot of gay people in it. Writers, all the arts. I mean, everyone's always known that. It's no big news. I guess the difference [during the Provincetown days] was that you read about it. People wrote books about it, which they hadn't in the past. That was changing along with everything else, with every kind of moral value and every other thing that was being knocked down. It was another visible rebellion.

> *Being eccentric has always been part of my career. I do that for a living. It's my job.*

IVES: So you've never felt ghettoized in any way?

WATERS: No. That may be politically incorrect to say, but I haven't. If I worked in an office somewhere, I might. But I have never been in that position. Being eccentric has always been part of my career. I do that for a living. It's my job. And the audiences have never been ghettoized, either. Thank God, gay people generally like my films, but they also play in places like universities all the time. It has been all types of audiences. Malcontents of all sexualities are who I count on. I get mail from all kinds of people, mostly people who say how happy they are that my sense of humor is like theirs. That's...the main thing they seem to identify with. Not sexuality. Sexuality is not the main focus of my films. Maybe it seemed that way because Divine was in it, but Divine was just the best actor I had, so he played a woman. I never really thought that was a comment on anything. To me, he was just a good actor who I built a lot of films around. And I liked making Divine/John Waters vehicles together.

IVES: Don't you think that added another element, another layer that strengthened what you were doing with him?

WATERS: Yes, because we didn't do the cliches of a drag queen. Divine was not about to sit around and do a Carol Channing imitation. He would stab to death someone who did. (Laughs.) Drag queens didn't like Divine, in the beginning. They hated him, because they knew he was making fun of them. They wanted to look pretty and

Waters (front row, center) said that the atmosphere on the Cry-Baby set was the happiest of all of his productions.

he was purposely looking hideous. But he turned that into a kind of beauty. It was just another reversal of a cliche. Divine didn't want to be a woman. He said it was so much trouble. In the end, he hated getting in drag. He only did it for movies and the nightclub act. But he always said it was an ordeal. He wasn't a natural beauty. I stayed with a friend (David Spencer) whom we all used to live with in San Francisco, and he said, "You know what I found when I was cleaning out my cellar?" And he showed me Divine's "cheater," which is a fake vagina that he wore under see-through dresses. I said, "You have to give that to Wesleyan." He said, "I will. I'll leave it with his pocketbook in a bureau." Divine's pocketbook and his cheater.... [Long, sad moment of nostalgic irony.]

IVES: You've got Ricki Lake in a couple of movies. Are you interested in building up a new repertory group?

WATERS: Well, not consciously, but I certainly want Ricki to be in my new movie. There's something about her that lends itself very well to my movies. And she brings something to my movies that I never had before: a basic inner cheerfulness. That is almost the opposite of what my characters are usually built on. I think of her as a Dreamland girl, one of the newest ones. It would be weird to make a movie without her now.

IVES: Would you like to have a new Dreamland group?

WATERS: No, that'll never be. At least not like the old days.

IVES: The second generation?

WATERS: There can be second generation, certainly. There already is. Pat's son, Brook, works in movies in L.A. now, and he's married to Traci Lords. People's kids work for us now. I really like that.

IVES: Yeah, because you can go in one of two directions—or both. The other is what you've been doing: bizarre against-type Hollywood casting.

WATERS: Liz Renay was the first of that. And Tab Hunter. They cost a little more, but they were the first stars I used outside of my friends. I still like that. The cameo casting in *Cry-Baby* was a gimmick, like Odorama.

IVES: It's a gimmick, but it works. Pia Zadora and Ric Ocasek as beatniks? That was great.

WATERS: Yeah, thanks. I want to work with Pia again. I really like her, just because she's Pia Zadora. Just that is enough.

IVES: But you're not actively thinking about trying to develop new actors to be part of your troupe?

WATERS: I always hope that will happen.

IVES: Do you see writing as your most important function?

WATERS: It's the part of it I enjoy the most. I like writing a book just as much as making a movie. And I can probably even be more completely myself when writing a book because editors don't say you have to play it to Peoria in a shopping mall. You can have a hit book even if it only sells in New York and L.A. That can be a best-seller. But movies are my first love, just because I've done that the most.

IVES: Are you going to write more books?

WATERS: Yeah. I always consider that as my second career. I still do journalism when they call and ask me. I like doing it. I'll write another book, I hope.

IVES: What happened during that seven years you didn't make movies?

WATERS: *Flamingos Forever*. I spent way too long trying to get it made when nobody would give me the money. Then I wrote *Crackpot*.

IVES: Wasn't *Crackpot* a collection of articles you had written?

WATERS: It started as that, but then I wrote more articles specifically for the book and then sold them to magazines.

IVES: When you're writing, other than for movies, what is the process? Your reviews you write, for instance?

WATERS: Sometimes I've found a book I really love, and I've called up the *New York Times*—because they have asked me to do stuff for them—and said, "I really want to [review] this book," and they've said, "Okay...." And when I was traveling in Europe promoting *Cry-Baby*, I found this art book I loved, and English *Vogue* had been asking me to do something, so I said, "Okay, let me do an art review," and they said yes. I save up my obsessions, and I like to only praise stuff. I don't like to write mean reviews, unless it's something that everyone else loves but really gets on my nerves. But even then, saying negative things doesn't look good in print.

> *I'm not a critic. As a writer, I'm much more comfortable praising things other people hate. That's sort of my specialty.*

IVES: Critics don't seem to mind.

WATERS: But I'm not a critic. As a writer, I'm much more comfortable praising things that other people hate. That's sort of my specialty.

IVES: Do you draw ideas for mischief in your films from your own childhood?

WATERS: Certainly. And from what I hear about other people's childhoods. Remember "Backwards Day" in *Desperate Living?* We had "Backwards Day" at camp. I remember it being so surreal to me, because they really did everything backwards. They picked you up in reverse order. You had dinner first. But you didn't have to walk backwards. I exaggerated it for the movie. I'm sure there are many more examples.

IVES: What about Channing dressing up in *Pink Flamingos?*

WATERS: No, I didn't dress up, if that's what you mean. Only once, as a witch. If you want my total drag experience, that was it. I was the Wicked Witch once on Halloween when I was really, really young.

IVES: What about Divine and Crackers "sliming" the house [in *Pink Flamingos*]? That seems like a kid kind of thing.

WATERS: No. I never did that. But it is a juvenile thing. It's the same kind of thing when the two kids lick at each other's lollipops in *Cry-Baby*, then switch them and put them in each other's mouths. There are lots of those kinds of "oral adventures." But I have no idea where the licking scene in *Pink Flamingos* came from, cursing the house by licking everything. Cursing was all that religious stuff, and licking something was building up to a blow job. That's sort of obvious, I guess. But I never licked the house down. I won't name names on this, but I know people who have licked other people's belongings to curse them when they were arguing while making a movie.

IVES: Really?

WATERS: Yes. I know of at least two people who have practiced that curse in their real lives.

IVES: They got the idea from *Pink Flamingos?*

WATERS: On *Cry-Baby* as adults, yeah...

IVES: You seem to get inspiration from friends a great deal, too.

WATERS: Oh, Pat! Pat [Moran] really is one of my best sources for funny lines. She gives me funny ideas all the time. I talk to her on the phone ten times a day. I've known her forever. She's my best buddy.

IVES: Do you bounce ideas off of her when you're writing?

WATERS: Yeah.

IVES: But she doesn't read your stuff until you're finished writing it, does she?

WATERS: No. Nobody does.

IVES: So you don't ever get reaction readings from people...

WATERS: ...No...

IVES: ...until you feel that it's done?

WATERS: Yeah. Then I do because then I have to hear everybody's notes. But when I'm writing it, I'll tell Pat something, you know, I'll talk about things, like, "Today I did this...blah, blah, blah," and see if she laughs. Sometimes it's hard because it's out of context, but I certainly bounce ideas off of her.

IVES: Are there other people you do that with?

WATERS: Dennis [Dermody], a friend of mine in New York. I talk to him all the time. And my agent [Bill Block], but not until I've thought it up and sent it to him. Then he tells me what he thinks. And when I go out there to pitch, I go into his office and pitch him first.

IVES: To see how it works?

WATERS: Yeah. This is today. In the old days I didn't do pitches. We just shot the movie. I never had notes from anybody. Ever. It was a first draft.

IVES: You didn't do rewrites?

WATERS: No, never, except maybe just a little in *Polyester*.

IVES: Do you do rewrites now?

WATERS: Oh, yeah. A lot. I did four or five drafts of *Cry-Baby*.

IVES: Are you a perfectionist about it?

WATERS: Yes. It's like a book. Even the commas have to be exactly right. I hand-write it all and Colleen types it—we're so modern now—on the word processor. But when I proofread, if I get a page and there's one comma wrong, I get her to change it. I turn out a very clean manuscript.

IVES: But I mean, are you a perfectionist about getting all the story lines right?

WATERS: Yes. I try to make sure it's consistent all the way through. But I always know everything is too long. I always overwrite and then cut.

IVES: How long do they usually come out?

WATERS: Well, the first one I do—which no one sees—is about one hundred and forty typewritten pages, which shocked me because it means my handwriting has shrunk since *Hairspray*. I used to know how many legal pad pages came out to a typewritten page, so I thought this one was probably going to be ninety-five pages long. Then she typed it and it was one hundred and forty.

IVES: Do your scripts follow the general rule of a minute a page?

WATERS: Usually they're longer than that because I write dense pages and I also have a lot of description in them, like exactly what every person is supposed to do. It was hard to tell with *Cry-Baby* because it was a musical. That threw it off. The final shooting script was probably ninety pages long, and I cut a half-hour out of it. So the minute-a-page rule doesn't work with me.

IVES: Do you ever have readings, when you get friends or actors you know to read it through and see how it sounds, so you can make changes?

WATERS: No. I have readings the week before we shoot. In the old days, we used to rehearse the whole thing like a play, for two months, because there were a lot of people like Edith Massey who needed rehearsal. But now, with most everybody professional, one week is enough.

IVES: I meant reading as part of the writing process. Some people do that. They write a script and they have people read...

WATERS: No, but I play every character sometimes. I did that on *Hairspray.* I read the whole script. I do that with every magazine article I write. I read it on tape, then I listen to it. And then I'll see if I'm using a word twice or something like that. That's the final step before I give it to Colleen to type. I talk to myself a lot when I'm writing dialogue; I say it out loud.

> *I talk to myself a lot when I'm writing dialogue; I say it out loud.*

IVES: Can you imagine ever collaborating with anyone?

WATERS: No. But in *Cry-Baby*, Jim Abrahams was the executive producer, which I never had before. What he did was good. He was like a book editor. We went through the script, and he would just question some things, which was good. He never said, "You should do this!" But as far as myself and another person sitting down and writing a script together, I can't imagine it. I'm too opinionated. I guess when I turn in a script they could hire another director. I really don't ever worry about that—who are they going to get? (Laughs.)

IVES: When you direct, do you tell everybody exactly how you want each character to sound?

WATERS: I used to in the old days, but now I have professional actors, and professional actors hate that more than anything in the whole world. I like cold-reading stuff, when they don't know anything about it. They come in, I hand it to them, and they have to do it. I can tell right away if they get it. In the old days, I would play every character.

IVES: You would tell everybody exactly how to do it and sort of act it out for them?

WATERS: Yeah. But I don't do that anymore, not even with the people

Waters says that Traci Lords looks like Patty McCormack (The Bad Seed) grown up. Lords played a sexy teen-ager in Cry-Baby.

I used to do it with. Like Mink.

IVES: Well, she's been with you so long that she probably knows.

WATERS: That's why I say that. I don't have to do anything. She knows exactly what I want. And I didn't do that with Divine in *Hairspray*. If I do any direction, it's to calm them down a little, because they like to, you know, chew up the scenery. I certainly didn't play the part with Johnny Depp on *Cry-Baby*, but on some lines I would direct him. We never had any arguments about it or anything. I get along with actors. I don't think any of them felt I was being an abusive director. I always knew exactly what I wanted in their performance, and if they were doing it wrong, I said so. But not meanly. I'm not like Otto Preminger. (Chuckles.)

IVES: You don't humiliate people?

WATERS: No. But the director in [*Glamourpuss*] does. The villain is the director. He's the biggest asshole there could be. That was fun to write, because it's the opposite of what I hope people think I'm like.

IVES: There's a game out called "Hollywood." Have you seen it? The object of the game is to make as much money as possible and to be as obnoxious and as much of an asshole as possible. You're supposed to steal and cheat and lie. And it comes with these little booklets that explain how to be an asshole.

> *The prisoners thought I was nuts—that's why they liked me. And that's why they trusted me.*

WATERS: No, I haven't seen that game, but I've seen some of that behavior. I've heard more stories about it than actually seen it. And there are actors I've heard so many horror stories about that I don't care how good they are, I ain't working with them. Life's too short.

IVES: Why do you like to teach in jail?

WATERS: Maybe I need to be in jail once a month. Makes me happy. Keeps me really interested, and I always feel like exhilarated when I leave. I still go in once in a while as a guest teacher. I go at least once a semester. I like to be around criminality sometimes.

IVES: But you have a good rapport with them?

WATERS: Oh yeah, they like me. I'm locked in a classroom with thirty of them. There's no guard.

IVES: They don't find you too bizarre or anything?

WATERS: When I taught the first lesson, I would make them stand up and do improv: "Okay, you just met your sister and she's had a sex change and she's a man." Some of them would be really uptight. But the ones that were really uptight dropped the class. The rest of them thought I was nuts—that's why they liked me. And that's why they trusted me. And they knew that I had no say about whether they got out of jail or not, so they could tell me the truth. So I tried to be good, to be...

IVES: ...a good teacher?

WATERS: Yes. And to not do anything that would be bad for them, for their rehabilitation. That's what I was supposed to be there for. So I took it fairly seriously. I think they liked the class. We made a movie on video there, but we had to erase it.

IVES: Why'd you have to erase it?

WATERS: Because that was part of the deal, and I get it. First of all it was so primitive—all we had was a video deck and a playback. There was no editing. Black-and-white. So, if I had taken it out and shown it, it would really be exploiting these prisoners. And they didn't want the other prisoners to see it, because some of the stuff they would do for me in class, they didn't want other prisoners to see. They reversed everything, you know—the blacks played the rich people, the bikers played girls. So everything was reversed against what their images were in jail. And they got into it as long as it was just us. But they would hang stuff on the door so the guards couldn't see.

IVES: So, let's segue to some of the fantasies in your films. What is their importance?

WATERS: Oh, *huge*. I make jokes on fantasies a lot. What kind of fantasies are you talking about? I have all kinds.

IVES: You've used lots of them. Going way back, you had Cinderella. You had all the Jesus Christ fantasies. In your last film, you had a flying biker chick. In *Flamingos Forever*, you had Divine with electric eyes and other weird things. She'd levitate.

WATERS: Oh, yeah, yeah, yeah. Well, that was just that she was so angry, she became almost cartoonish.

IVES: She was like the Sea Witch [in *Little Mermaid*].

WATERS: Yeah, she was ranting so heavily, she just went off the ground. And Divine could have done that great, too. A lot of times you can have fantasies that are very good, but in real life they're not too healthy. But in movies, I try to make fun of fantasies. I try to think of funny fantasies. And believe me there is nothing you can think of that someone hasn't had as a real fantasy. I have read a lot of books about criminology. I've read all of Freud. I read a lot of books on weirdness. *Autoerotic Fatalities* is a book that I find really amazing, because there's stuff in there that shocks me, that makes me think, "God, I feel so healthy." (Laughs.) I think, "Look what they have to go through to have an orgasm?" They have to have all these props and all this, you know? But I don't judge that; it fascinates me. Especially if you exaggerate it and turn it into humor.

IVES: I don't mean just sex fantasies, although, obviously you include those....

WATERS: Well, all the movies are fantasies. Dawn Davenport's fantasy was to be famous as a criminal. My movies are about fame a lot. Hallie [Harriotte Aaron], my script supervisor [on *Cry-Baby*], said to me last time, "No one has a private life in this movie". I never thought of it that way, but in some way, the whole fame thing is surreal—and it's so important in America. This happened to me the other night, it was a perfect example of the ludicrousness of fame. A married couple I've known for twenty years, Judith and Bob Pringle, were visiting me, staying at my house. We went out to Club Charles and, afterwards, we stopped at the 7-ELEVEN. Judith was sitting in the front seat with me, and Bob, her husband, was in the back. Judith sat in the car while Bob and I went in the 7-ELEVEN. I bought something and walked out to the car, but Bob was still in there paying for something. Someone said, "Look, there's John Waters." They all looked, and then someone else said, "Yeah, look, he's with a prostitute". (Laughs.) Judith, my old friend, they thought was a prostitute. People will say anything. That's how these kind of rumors get started. The whole fame thing is funny to me. And that's in all of my movies in some way. Johnny Depp is a famous singer.

IVES: Ricki Lake becomes a famous...

WATERS: ...famous TV dancer. Dawn Davenport becomes a famous criminal. Divine was already famous retired [in *Pink Flamingos*], trying to live her life in filth and peace....

IVES: Do you read fairy tales?

WATERS: As a kid, I liked some of them. I liked "Slovenly Peter," the German one, where they cut off his hands. I liked "Chicken Little" a lot. Certain ones I still think about. Like I wonder if the sky will fall. (Laughs.) Certain little moments have influenced me heavily, but I'm not a buff.... I liked them as a kid, and when I did the puppet shows I did "Cinderella." I used it in *Mondo Trasho*.

IVES: Well, you sort of used it in *Desperate Living*, didn't you? It was definitely in one of your other films.

WATERS: Yeah. It seems like it was to me, too. Maybe the Foot Stomper [in *Polyester*] was Prince Charming gone in the other direction. But there was a real foot stomper.... There were a couple of them. And one of them serves his time, and then the parole board says, "Are you gonna do this again?" and he says, "I swear, Judge, I'm not." Then they catch him doing it again two days later. I feel bad for him. To him that's normal. Instinct. He has to go step on people's feet, and there's no way he can ever do that really. You know? It still gets reported on the news for the same reason people laugh about it in the movie, because it's so quirky. But then sometimes I think of being him. Just think what would it be like if I did that in a shopping mall? But that's a kind of thing I don't act on.

IVES: But as a filmmaker you can use all that.

WATERS: You can do it, yeah. That's what I said before: I don't know what would have happened with all these things that are in my mind if I didn't make movies.

IVES: You also have had some recurring symbols.

WATERS: I'll give you my best Freudian analysis now. What's that test called? Where they say a word, and you say the first thing that comes to your mind? Free association.

IVES: Chickens.

WATERS: Chickens. I think when I was a kid I was frightened by a chicken. I still think they're hideous. But I look back at [*Mondo Trasho*], at killing them, and I'm shocked that I ever filmed that. That's the most hideous thing I ever filmed. I would understand people being upset about that. Because we didn't even eat those chickens. Now, the chickens we killed in *Pink Flamingos*, we ate.

IVES: You mean the execution in the beginning of *Mondo Trasho*?

WATERS: Yes. That is horrible. I was trying to do a joke on *Mondo Cane*. That was pre-PETA [People for the Ethical Treatment of Animals]. (Laughs.) But it's something I'm a little ashamed of, because it was really cruel. I just can't look at it when it comes on. Chickens were a sexual thing in *Pink Flamingos*. I never had any real-life sexual fantasies about chickens. I know what you're thinking but not that either. I'm not a chicken queen either. (Laughs.)

IVES: No, no, I wasn't thinking that.

WATERS: Anything that frightens me I always use a lot. I think.

IVES: What about foot fetishes?

Waters insists that sex is made to look ludicrous in all of his films. Mary Vivian Pearce and David Lochary cavort (above) in Multiple Maniacs.

WATERS: Well, I told you before, I'm not...shrimping to me is the most ludicrous-looking sex act. That's why I used it. And it has the Cinderella influence. It has a lot of history, that whole thing. I like shoes, but, I mean, I don't lick them. I want to *buy* them.

IVES: I'm not trying to get at whether you do these things; I'm trying to get at why they're in your films.

WATERS: I know. The shoe fetish thing is an influence of Bunuel. He had that in *Viridiana*, one of my all-time favorite movies. I've never thought of that before; this [interview] is like going to the shrink. I watched that movie again recently. Maybe that is where the seeds of it came from. It's been in a lot of movies. It's a fetish I can understand. I mean, it's not totally foreign to me. Cinderella was, you know, trying the shoe on. That was the first movie I ever saw: Walt Disney's *Cinderella*. I played the record over and over and over. Especially when the stepmother comes and says, "Cinderella..." and the music goes Da-DADA-Da-DADA. I still have the record. It's an old warped seventy-eight. Da-DADA-Da-DADA-Da-DADA-Da DADA. I wanted that music to play whenever I stepped into a room for the rest of my life.

IVES: What about fat women?

WATERS: The biggest influence on me was Saraghina in *8 1/2*. And the mother in *The Loved One*. Those are my fat influences. Loving those two characters and the Russ Meyer women—put together—came up with Divine.

IVES: But Divine isn't the only fat woman in your films. There are a lot of them.

WATERS: Divine certainly started it.

IVES: You had Jean Hill and you had Ricki Lake and...

WATERS: Yeah. On some occasions I do feel like Jack Sprat. That's another fairy tale that I identified with. People have asked me a lot if I am turned on by fat people. I'm not. I mean, I'm not a chubby chaser. But I love those characters very, very much. Saraghina was an influence on Edith's character, too. Saraghina lived in an old shack on the beach, and the kids would come to her and they were scared of her but, you know? Divine could scare kids more than Edie...the mother in *The Loved One* was a little Edithesque. All she wanted was food all the time. My favorite scene was when she pulled the whole refrigerator on top of her.

IVES: Fellini had a lot of fat women. *Satyricon* had a lot of them, and

Amarcord, and I can't remember whether *I Vitelloni* did, but that was like *Amarcord One.*

WATERS: Yes it was. *8 1/2* and *La Dolce Vita* were big influences on me. I was young enough when I saw them that they were huge influences. I must have seen *8 1/2* ten times. It is one of my favorite films. There's one scene where the director comes and the starlet is walking down these marble steps and I always think it's in the Carlton [in Cannes] and I have to wonder, "Well is it?" It's some big hotel. And I think of that every time I walk down those steps in the Carlton. My very favorite thing is that each step has an ad on it. That's the only ad I want. One stair on the Carlton stairway. I'm really impressed by that. Whoever advertises gets their dollar's worth with me, because I stop and look at it and think, "Oh, *this* is what show business is all about." Real estate! When you sit down at those tables in Cannes [at the film festival] and pay twenty dollars, you're not eating lunch—you're paying rent on that table for an hour to talk to these people. There are eight people in the world who could say yes to you making a movie, and three of them are there. That's not a food bill, that's a real estate bill. (Chuckles.)

IVES: What about angels in your earlier stuff?

WATERS: Well, that was Catholicism, of course. You know, I used to believe the Easter Bunny was a guardian angel, that they were one and the same. That was my schizophrenia as a child: mixing up saints with capitalistic selling points. I would forget if I was supposed to pray to Santa Claus or Jesus. They seemed to me to be sort of the same. I like the idea of angels. I don't know that I necessarily believe in them, but I like the idea of them. I had them in *Mondo Trasho,* but somebody would just appear to people and start ranting religiously. But the most touching thing happened to me when Divine died—a fan printed up a holy card of Divine with that prayer on the back and sent it to me. It really made me cry.

IVES: That prayer was unbelievable.

WATERS: I had forgotten it.

IVES: Lend me the plenary strength or...

WATERS: The plenary indulgence. Well, the plenary indulgence always upsets me because in the Catholic church you could murder fifty people and go in and say this prayer, and it would wipe out all your guilt and time in hell.

IVES: Didn't people buy those in the Middle Ages?

WATERS: Yes. Before the Reformation. My hobby. One of the main things that toppled papal administrations was the sale of indulgences. But that kind of angel in the movie was usually someone coming in and doing some sort of religious rant. Even Mink in the "rosary job." That was not an angel but that was like what would happen if you were untruthful. I used to sit in church and imagine explosions, the roof falling in, every horrible thing that could happen...everybody would say "*ARGHH*," running out like Gorgo stepping on [things]. You know? I would fantasize that because I was bored. And they made us stand up and take the Legion Of Decency Pledge that we wouldn't go see these condemned movies. That was the first thing that I refused to do. And that led me to everything. Because every week I looked at the Legion of Decency. I looked at every title—*Love Is My Profession, The Bed, Mom and Dad, Naked Night*—and I'd think, "God, this is so *great*."

IVES: Who came up with those lists?

WATERS: Who knows? It was put out every week. They still have it!

IVES: How did they know what was in the movies? Did they go and look at them?

WATERS: Yeah. The Legion of Decency screened them. In the fifties and sixties they ruined *Baby Doll*. That was the main movie they went after. They were like the rating board now. They still have it, but now "O" for offensive. Condemned is better. You hear that big iron brand hit metal with smoke sizzling out: "Condemned!" I always wanted to be condemned, and I don't think I ever was because they would never even bother submitting my films. Why waste the postage? I think *Polyester* was the first one that they ever submitted, and that got a B— morally offensive in part or all. I was really disappointed.

IVES: Are you religious?

WATERS: No. I believe that there is maybe *something*, but I'll never, ever know what it is. There's a word for that. Is that agnostic?

IVES: I guess.

WATERS: Well, that's what I believe. There could be something. I mean how did all this happen? That's fascinating to me, but I don't think any human knows yet what it is. I'm certainly against organized religion that judges other people's morals. I like the excesses of the Catholic Church, though. It certainly formed me. If I had a child, I would not raise it Catholic. Looking back at my high school, I think they were guilty of child abuse. Mental and physical. I saw them beat people up. The nuns I had in Sunday School were insane, devious, sick sadists. They were like she-wolves. Ilsa, the Mother of God. I've used all that, but I agree with Madonna when she said that Catholicism is a mean religion. And they teach that it is good to have guilt, and I find that so fucked up. But interesting, because Jews have shame and Catholics have guilt—it's real close.

The nuns I had in Sunday School were insane, sick, devious sadists. They were like she-wolves.

IVES: Well, Jews have guilt, too, but it's a different kind of guilt. It's not cosmic guilt. It's a guilt like, "I should have called this person, I should have done that, I feel sorry I didn't do this, and I didn't do that, or I should have, I shouldn't have," you know? All that stuff is built into the Jewish character.

WATERS: Yes, but you're not taught that when you're born you have something that has to be wiped away. Original Sin.

IVES: No.

WATERS: Well that's the whole concept of the Catholic Church. It's just insane. But, in times of fear, I would certainly say everyone prays.

IVES: In some way.

WATERS: Yes, to something. So if that's being religious, I am. I'm not an atheist at all. I hope there is something. Because then a lot of things mean something. The worst thing to me—even worse than Catholicism—is the idea of reincarnation, that it's never over. I see people in the street and I think, "Suppose I come back? I have to live a hundred of these people's lives, for the rest of eternity?" That is a much more horrifying thought than Hell. (Laughs.) I know people who I think, "Thank God I'm not them." To wake up every day and feel the insanity that they feel would be worse than Hell. Fire? You get used to it being hot.

IVES: Are you conscious of being Catholic as—I know you hate the word—an artist, as a filmmaker?

WATERS: Yeah, I think so.

IVES: I mean you could argue that Scorsese in a way is a Catholic film-maker.

WATERS: So is Warhol. You can name all the Catholic ones. They're always the ones whose films I like very much. Pasolini...

IVES: Right, Fellini.

WATERS: Fellini, yes. So I am certainly a Catholic filmmaker. That doesn't mean that I'm a good Catholic. It taught me. The Catholic kids in the neighborhood were always the ones that got into the most trouble, because they told us more that we couldn't do this or that. So it has formed me, the same way that being gay has. I'm Catholic, I'm gay. Pasolini says it best: "I'm a Catholic, I'm a homosexual, I'm a communist..." and one other, I forget, but it was something that really enraged everybody. You can't look at early movies without seeing it, like the Infant of Prague walking across the street with Divine [in *Multiple Maniacs*]. How could I not be Catholic and do that?

There is no scene more blasphemous than the rosary job in any movie you can show me.

IVES: No, it seems like it's actually a theme that you really wanted to explore.

WATERS: It was, up until the rosary job. I'd like to think that got it out of my system, because there is no scene more blasphemous than that in any movie you can show me. And it still is really rude.

IVES: She's wiping it off with her sleeve.

WATERS: I know, and then to top it off with someone really shooting up on the altar. It was the most gratuitous shot in any of my movies. For no reason, just one other horrible thing. And he was shooting up for real. It was a little last-minute ad lib.

IVES: Like kicking the priest in the rear one more time?

WATERS: No. The priest let us do it but he didn't know what we were doing. He came though, and saw it. But he wasn't really angry. He just said, "Please don't ever tell anybody where you did it." And do you know, to this day I don't know where we filmed that?

IVES: You forgot?

WATERS: If I said, "Let's go right now, I'll show you that church," I wouldn't know where it was. I know where the outside was in the film, but that isn't really where we really filmed the inside. We went there at night. Howard [Gruber] took me there. (Laughs.) He knew the priest in some way.

IVES: Do you read Catholic writers? I know you're into, what is it?

WATERS: Extreme Catholic behavior before the Reformation...I don't consciously go out and get Catholic stuff—except books about the bad popes. And St. Catherine of Sienna is my mentor. She was the most insane of all of them. She ate scabs from cancer patients and offered them up to God. That's Catholic. (Laughs.) I mean?

She's in all the books about that extreme Catholic behavior. She is the pinup girl from that era, believe me.

IVES: Is this something that you will explore further in your films?

WATERS: I think it's pretty much over with. I also recognize that it's not very commercial, because if you're not Catholic, you won't get those jokes.... If you're not Catholic, do you get that the Infant of Prague was ludicrous because you changed his outfit every few months? It had four different outfits, you know, for the seasons. It was so obscure!... If you listen to the dialogue, he says his famous statement: "The more you honor me, the more I will bless you." I like the politics of that. (Laughs.)

IVES: Particularly coming from a little kid.

WATERS: Yes, in a ludicrous fashion outfit with a papal hat. (Laughs.) And in Baltimore, for some reason, the Infant of Prague is still very big in a lot of blue-collar neighborhoods. He's in a lot of windows. Pat's mother always had one when she was growing up, she said.

IVES: What about child abuse [in your films]?

WATERS: Well, I have it, but it's comic child abuse. In *Female Trouble*, I don't think anybody really feels bad for that little girl when Divine says, "You want another whipping with that car aerial?" Maybe I'm wrong.

IVES: Obviously, it's set within a humorous context; you're not sitting there thinking that you're watching a Bergman film. But, particularly when she's younger, she's not allowed to go outside and all of that. I mean, it was obviously an attempt to be extreme, but...

WATERS: ...but people always laughed at that. When she says, "If I hear one more jump rope chant." That was always humorous. To me that never even seemed that cruel. I don't think I've ever had child abuse in my movies. Now you can probably name twelve other examples of that, but I think it was done in the humorous spirit of the films. In *Female Trouble*, she had this horrible blue-collar, white-trash life until these beauticians paid attention to her and turned her into a star, even though it was worse than what she had before. That's what that movie was about, that notoriety and fame are really the same. I mean? *Female Trouble* was inspired by one Diane Arbus shot. It's a shot of a woman with a hairdo very much like Dawn Davenport's, with tadpole eyebrows, with like a retarded-looking husband, holding a drooling baby. Diane Arbus was a huge influence on me. I said in my book that I felt like that kid with the hand grenade all during my childhood. When I say that, people say, "Oh, he's out to lunch,"

Joe Dallesandro and Joey Heatherton played a stern Reverend and his wife in Cry-Baby.

but I meant that joyously. That kid looked like he was having fun to me. So, that's why that was in there, to show the horrors. Part of white-trash living, unfortunately, is child abuse. It's big there.

IVES: Well, what you see in the Dawn Davenport early years is that she's totally out of control and impossible and her parents seem fairly innocent, but if you stop and think about it for a minute, you've got to think that if this child is this bad, so completely out of control and insane that she would throw her mother under the Christmas tree because she didn't get cha-cha heels, maybe her parents did something awful to her. And then when she gets older, and she has a child...

WATERS: See, I never thought her parents did something awful to her. I guess I thought that it would be more interesting if her parents didn't do anything bad to her and she was just rotten.

IVES: Just a bad seed.

WATERS: Yes. *The Bad Seed* was my Christmas card one year. I have her picture in my bedroom, sitting right on my desk. That was a huge influence on me. Traci Lords looks like Patty McCormack. That's what Iggy Pop told me and I said, "You're right! I never even thought of that. It's like Patty McCormack grown up." So that's where that came from. Her parents were just so suburban. They were just like, "Come on Dawn, please." It was almost how I saw all of my friends' parents, like when Divine's parents said, "What are you thinking about?" They were so appalled at the shit we were doing that they'd just say, "How could you do this?" That's what I wanted to show. I didn't think of Divine's [Dawn Davenport's] parents as being white-trash child beaters; she became that because she was pregnant, she had no money—every horrible thing that could happen to a runaway girl happened to her. And then her daughter grew up to be a Hare Krishna, which is the worst thing a child could ever be. For our generation, with our values, it's maybe worse than having a kid in jail.

IVES: You said that in addition to your perfect legal pads and your pens, you had a notebook of titles and a notebook of cast.

WATERS: Yep. And a notebook of music.... But titles are sometimes the very first thing I think of. *Glamourpuss* was from two movies; I saw the word used in an article—I think in *GQ*, I'm embarrassed to admit—it just made me laugh... I have a back-up title, *Raving Beauty*, which works for it too. But *Glamourpuss* is a more obvious John Waters title, which is what they may fear... But I've had different titles for most of my movies. Back-up titles. *Hairspray* was *White*

Lipstick, Female Trouble was *Rotten Mind, Rotten Face. Desperate Living* was called *Mortville* for a while. They've all gone through different titles, but there's always one that sticks and says what the whole movie is. A title is so important. It has to be fun to say. Or it has to make you laugh just to say it.

IVES: It has to be catchy. And it should be short.

WATERS: Tennessee Williams had the best titles ever...like *Cat on a Hot Tin Roof.* What a great title. *Suddenly, Last Summer.* And, of course, my favorite thing of all is when they actually say the title in the movie. It makes me go crazy. Every time. I love it so much when they work it into the dialogue, when [one of the characters says], "...suddenly, last summer," or, "What's the matter with Helen?" When that happens, it makes me almost levitate.

IVES : Do you have a theory about your choice of music?

WATERS: Well, all my life I grew up with black music. I never liked the Beatles. To me, they ruined rock-and-roll. That's when I stopped liking rock-and-roll. And I didn't like it again until rap. I liked the idea of punks, but I didn't run out and buy all those albums. But I've always liked all kinds of music—you know? I like classical music; I don't know a lot about it, but it's like what the Supreme Court says about porno: They know it when they see it.

IVES: Right.

WATERS: I always grew up on black radio stations, with rhythm and blues. Baltimore had three great black stations: WSID, WEBB, and WWIN. They were really, really good. All the white kids listened to the black music in Baltimore. The cool ones...I mean, *Cry-Baby* was basically about that. So was *Hairspray*. My mentor for music in movies was

My mentor for music in movies was Kenneth Anger.

Kenneth Anger, who employed the ironic use of pop music before anyone else. He did that in *Scorpio Rising*, which was a huge influence on me. Martin Scorsese copied him. Every filmmaker—including me—copied him. He [Anger] changed music in movies. I use music in the same way as the novelty record *Flying Saucer*. It told a story by taking bits of music [and interspersing it with spoken dialogue]. "Meanwhile, we go downtown..." (Sings.) "Come on, baby, let's go downtown." (Speaks again.) "This is a flying saucer." And then part of a Little Richard song, you know? They'd steal a lot; it was the first sampling there was. Of course, it wasn't called that, but they would use ten seconds of a song. And I use that to tell my stories; in *Cry-Baby* they cut to a jail and you hear, (sings) "He's in the jailhouse now. He's in the jailhouse now." Fade out. I use music as narration and bridging scenes and that kind of thing. That's what all soundtracks do. But I do it more vocally, to tell the story. And in *Cry-Baby* I thought up whole scenes because the music came first. For *Glamourpuss*, I turned in a whole soundtrack with twenty-six songs. I listen to music the whole time I'm writing.

IVES: Do you have the music in mind while you're writing?

WATERS: Sometimes. With *Hairspray* I did. And *Cry-Baby*. But I listened to all music from that period. I have this guy in Baltimore named Larry Benicewicz, who literally owns every record that's ever been put out in any form of music. That's all his house is—just records. He is insane with records. So I tell him, "I want every song you can think of. Here's a subject." I want the lyrics to actually be about the subject or about the opposite of the subject. He gives me tape after tape, and I listen to them and make notes. Then I get it down to the first seventy-five I liked, the first fifty, the first twenty. Then it comes down to what I do, and that's not the score, it's the vintage music....

IVES: Is the music in *Cry-Baby* accurate?

WATERS: Mm-hm. Completely accurate.

IVES: Some of it seemed like it was way past 1954.

WATERS: No, none of it is, except there's a cheat, two of them. "The Bad Boy" is '55. Big deal. It's all from that exact period. It's correct. It was rock-a-billy, which was before rock-and-roll....We redid a couple of songs, like the one they sing outside the jail when they're on the phone. There was a song called "Please Mr. Jailer" by somebody else, and I changed the lyrics to be more towards the plot. The music has always been used either ironically to make a point or to tell part of the story as a narrator would do. It's the *Flying Saucer* school of soundtracks.

IVES: Sometimes quite blatantly, jumping from one thing to the next.

WATERS: Yeah, and it tells like exactly what happened in [the] one lyric I snatch out of a song.

IVES: Are there any musicians you'd like to score your films?

WATERS: Well, I told the music supervisor on *Cry-Baby* all the names, and he came back to me and said, "They're all in one place: Forest Lawn." They're all dead.

IVES: So how do you pick somebody? I mean, you do have a score in addition to music.

WATERS: My music supervisors [on *Cry-Baby*], Becky Mancuso and Tim Sexton, brought me a lot of people, different ages, with different stuff, you know? And I just had to take a hunch from what they had done. It's always just, "Do they get it?" How do you know that until they do it? But the music part is fun. *Cry-Baby* was the first time I was actually in there with an orchestra playing. A whole union orchestra scoring a scene with a click track. [*A click track is a soundtrack on which a series of clicks have been recorded, picked up by the conductor's headphones, to indicate the desired tempo during post-recording of the film's score.—JI*] That was amazing. It was something I'd always wanted to do.

IVES: Well, you're now working with a full technical crew. When you were just starting out, you didn't have much money and you were trying to do things a certain way, but you didn't have the ability to do it.

WATERS: Not even the ability, I didn't know you *could* do it.

IVES: But how do you compare it? I mean, there are probably plusses and minuses to doing everything on your own.

WATERS: Oh, a lot of plusses.

IVES: Or having people around to do them.

WATERS: On *Hairspray* there was one scene—we had gotten all the permits and everything—and we had to get this one pick-up shot that didn't work out. They told us we couldn't because there was traffic, it was rush hour. We just jumped out and did it. It was kind of thrilling. That was like the old days. But when I was doing it in the beginning, I didn't even know about any other way.

IVES: Well, everybody knew that there were movie factories out in Hollywood and that there were crews and things like that.

WATERS: Yeah, but in those years, when I made *Hag in a Black Leather Jacket*, this is how much I knew: I sent ads for it to try to get the drive-in to book it, not knowing that a drive-in couldn't show an 8-mm movie. I didn't know anything. I actually thought there was a possibility, because it sold out once in a coffee shop with thirty people who just said, "Huh?" And I passed the hat.

IVES: But primarily you made films the way you did in the beginning out of necessity. You wanted to make films, but you didn't have any money, so you just figured out a way to do it.

WATERS: Yes, but that was because the underground film movement had told me that you could do that. I don't know that I would have done it if I hadn't read about that movement. I used to think on LSD: "I can do that." I'd tell my parents that and they'd just say, "That's the most horrible thing I've ever heard." It's the opposite of what you're supposed to say about drugs, you know, "LSD gave me the confidence to do it." (Chuckles.) Politically incorrect.

IVES: But if you're doing a film for, say, Paramount, even if you're working with lower budgets than someone else might, don't you still have to do certain things certain ways?

WATERS: You have to make the slickest movie you can make.

IVES: But do you have to have a certain number of crew and different people doing certain things? Would you like to work with a smaller group or somehow trim things down?

WATERS: It depends on the movie. *Cry-Baby* was really big sometimes, cumbersomely big. But I can't think of anyone there who wasn't doing something. You always wish you had a little more money, because the thing you need is time. There's not enough time in the shooting day to get all the shots you want. That's what the money is about. Even with *Cry-Baby*. You have all this stuff you planned to shoot that day, then you get there and see the sun. You see the hours, you realize you're not going to be able to get the coverage for every shot you want, so you compromise. Everyone does that. *Terminator 2* did it. That's hard to imagine, but...

> *We shot Mondo Trasho in laundromats because they had fluorescent lighting. That's why I always wrote laundromat scenes—you didn't need light.*

IVES: What did you do about lighting in your early films?

WATERS: Well, we shot *Mondo Trasho* in laundromats, because they had fluorescent lighting. That's why I always wrote laundromat scenes— you didn't need light. I had one sun gun as they were called. You know what they are? You can put them in cars, they used them a lot, just pointing up towards the person.

IVES: You mean those things that went on the outside of the car?

WATERS: No, just something you held. On *Mondo Trasho*, I don't think we ever had lights. We had one light inside, the kind you got at a store for home movies. I probably borrowed it from my parents. *Multiple Maniacs* was the same way. We had a light—one. We used it with a long extension cord. Just one bright light that lit the room, whatever we could get. That's why *Mondo Trasho* was mostly shot outside. We just didn't have any lights.

IVES: When did you start using real lighting? Of course, not totally real, but more real?

WATERS: Well, it was gradual. *Female Trouble* was the first one that had more than one light. *Pink Flamingos* had one light. *Female Trouble* was the first time we did any kind of lighting. That was the first one that had a real crew. Three or four people.

IVES: But you had somebody doing lighting in *Female Trouble*?

WATERS: Yeah. That wasn't their only job. It wasn't until *Female Trouble* that we had a Nagra. *[A Nagra is a small, portable audiotape recorder used on location.—JI]* On *Pink Flamingos*, I wore the earphones; I heard the dialogue the whole time, right when it was going on the film on the magnetic stripe.

IVES: And what kind of camera did you use in *Female Trouble*?

WATERS: *Female Trouble* and *Desperate Living* were 16-mm; we blew them up. It wasn't until *Polyester* that we had a 35-mm.

IVES: When did you start using a DP [director of photography] or a cameraman?

WATERS: *Desperate Living*. I had a cameraman, Tom Loizeaux, but I actually pushed the button and looked through the viewfinder. They weaned me away from that—correctly, God knows—in *Desperate Living*. But I still have to have video; I have to see it.

IVES: Is that what you do now?

WATERS: Oh, yes. I couldn't do it without that.

IVES: Are you right there on the set with the video?

WATERS: I'm right on the set. But I generally watch the actual shot on the TV screen with earphones. Sometimes I don't, but mostly I do. Then I get up and direct.

IVES: When did you start doing that?

WATERS: *Polyester*.... It was the first time I ever knew about it, or I would have demanded it all along.

IVES: Have you ever had any interest in using black-and-white again?

WATERS: No. I just did it then because I couldn't afford color. It's almost pretentious to make a black-and-white movie now, unless you're Scorsese. He's the best American filmmaker. But for any other director, it's reverse snobbism. I think it's silly. It's the emperor's new clothes. Like letter box. What is the point? I never understood why you have 1.85 either. Why don't you fill whatever it is?

Waters behind the camera reviewing a shot in Desparate Living.

I don't get that. I mean, I know I have to do it that way, so I do it. I don't understand why you'd have a letter box on a TV screen. So part of the screen isn't filled?

IVES: Well, all of that will go away when they have new-shaped TV screens. Have you ever used Cinemascope?

WATERS: No, it just makes it harder to show. It's hard enough to get my movies in theaters. I don't want to give them any technical excuses not to. Godard used it in *Contempt*. I love him. I love *King Lear*. And I really like his latest ones. They were really dirty there for awhile. Did you see like *Every Man for Himself*? I like that period of Godard a lot. They were filthy.

IVES: Filthy and very strange.

WATERS: And so good... What was the other one called?

IVES: *Detective*.

WATERS: Yeah, I loved that one too. I love all that period.

IVES: I found that a little hard to follow.

WATERS: Well, of course, you can't follow them. I love when he's in them, like in *King Lear* with telephone extension cords hanging from his head. I thought, "Hmm, that's a nice look."

IVES: You have regular crew people from the old days who are still with you.

WATERS: Rachel Talalay—who produced my last two movies—was a free PA [production assistant] on *Polyester*. If there's ever a reason to say, "To get in the movie business, you should go work on a movie for free," that's it. That is how you get in the movie business. Go work for free

> *To get in the movie business, you should go work on a movie for free.*

somewhere and, if everybody likes you, you get paid on the next job and then you're in. I mean, it's not easy. We fire free people. Just because you work for free doesn't mean you aren't going to get a lot of shit, too. But that is the way to get in. Every one of us—including me—learned by making these movies.

IVES: And Pat Moran and Van Smith.

WATERS: Yeah, and Vince Peranio—they all got a little more money each time, but they did great jobs even when they got no money.

IVES: Did some of them work other places?

WATERS: They all do.

IVES: And that doesn't bother you?

WATERS: It's better for me. Within the studio system, they're always suspicious of people who have only worked for me. So I love it when they work for other people. It makes it easier for me to say, "Of course, I'm using this person."

IVES: Did things change when you started shooting with 35-mm?

WATERS: It changed. *Polyester* was three hundred and some thousand dollars. That seemed, at the time, like we were really big-time. But, did it change the feeling? No.

IVES: Didn't it change the way you approached the material or anything?

WATERS: No. That one was really hard to film. I think there were twenty shooting days. Maybe less. Ten? I don't even remember, but it was hard. It was horrible hours. We always did twenty-hour days in those old movies. We can't do that any more, with unions. Also, I was in my thirties then. But there were days when people just would start crying from exhaustion. On *Desperate Living*, it was horrible like that; we even forgot to have food on that movie. Some of the extras got touchy about that. (Laughs.)

IVES: Is that the film where Pat and Mink...

WATERS: They cooked.

IVES: But nobody would eat it.

WATERS: Well, Liz Renay said, "I don't like to say anything, but I was in Terminal Island prison and the food was better than this."

IVES: When did you start paying people?

WATERS: *Pink Flamingos.* My main eight people—to this day—get a total of twenty-five percent of every movie up until *Polyester*, when they got real pay. I mail the checks four times a year. Sometimes it's fifty bucks, sometimes it's a thousand—if there was a video deal, or something. That's not bad—twenty years later, these checks just come in the mail. Some people got paid on *Pink Flamingos*. I mean, maybe three hundred dollars, tops. I didn't get any salary. The percentage thing started to happen after it came out.

IVES: But you've made money on *Pink Flamingos*?

WATERS: Oh sure. I'm not complaining.

IVES: It took a while, though.

WATERS: Yeah, it did. And, believe me, I'm sure I made less than most people think.

IVES: You seem to inspire people to work with you, even when you haven't been able to pay them much.

WATERS: They were my friends, we hung around together. That was the thing. And that was the sixties; nobody even thought about having money. We weren't doing it to make money, we were doing it to get our sense of humor out. And I'm sure that all those people had the fantasy of being in movies, of being famous or being notorious.

IVES: But from all the articles I've read, it seems that people get very inspired by you somehow.

WATERS: Obsession is catching. You know? So if they see that I'm really into it, they get into it.

IVES: You become friends with a lot of them.

WATERS: Well, I think that's part of it. If you create a family-type atmosphere on a movie set, you'll get better performances. Spending four months with somebody under those conditions is like war. Being in a movie is like being in the military, in a way. You travel in packs and trucks. You set up camp. You take over neighborhoods. You know, you try to get away with stuff. (Laughs.) There's a certain bondedness that comes with that. And I always pick people that I respect. They know that.

IVES: And you treat them with respect.

WATERS: Yeah. I wouldn't ask Patty Hearst to play a bank robber, you see what I mean? I know it would be so rude to ask her to do that. But most people don't see the difference...

IVES: How did you get all of the extras in your movies?

WATERS: When?

IVES: Well, say, the middle period.

WATERS: Pat. And Edith helped a lot. Down by her store she'd have a sign up: "Want to come be an extra?" Pat would get them on a bus—where they couldn't escape—because once they got there and realized it was going to be twenty hours, there was no food and it was freezing, it was horrible.

IVES: Oh, and you would take the bus away?

WATERS: We'd make the bus leave and come back later. Pat always handled that for me.

IVES: And you didn't pay them?

WATERS: No. No one seemed to mind, I mean, they liked being in movies. I pay extras today, because it makes it easier. But there are people, even today, who would like to spend a whole day watching a movie being made. It is an education to see what it's like. And in those days, it wasn't about money. It was about being in a film that did well culturally. It wasn't such a big deal about which movie grossed how much, not like today. They didn't print the top ten grossing movies in the paper every week. It wasn't the hit parade. It was more like: "What trouble could our movie cause?" That's why people wanted to be extras in my movies. Or they liked Edith, or they rooted for our success outside of Baltimore. They were helping us. They liked the movie and they wanted to help by being in it. And I felt a kind of closeness with all of them...but, it's true that I'm nicer to extras. The thing I really don't understand about Hollywood rules is that the director isn't allowed to talk to the extras, which makes me crazy.

IVES: Why do you think that is?

WATERS: Well, I do talk to them, anyway. Mary Ellen [Woods, first assistant director on *Cry-Baby*] said she realized that a John Waters movie is the only film where there is no such thing as an extra. They're such a part of it. And I'll show close-ups of them and everything. So I would talk to them all; I just [was not allowed to] look at one of them specifically and tell them a specific thing to do or say.

IVES: Because then they stop being extras, contractually.

WATERS: Yeah. But extras are important, and I don't think our extras looked like extras, like they do in Hollywood. We got extras in Hollywood for one reshoot scene, and I thought they were a nightmare. I got every lunatic fan that wanted to be in it, but they didn't want to work for twenty hours straight. Here [in Baltimore], Pat finds extras who aren't dancers, and we train them because then they look so real. Like in the prison scene in *Cry-Baby*? I think they look like real prisoners. They certainly didn't look like the June Taylor dancers. Here [in Baltimore] they have people like that. That's why I like it here. That's why I make movies here.

IVES: I used to see all the Fellini films and I would think, "Where does he get these people?" Then I went to Italy and there they were, walking around on the streets.

WATERS: It's like that here in Baltimore. I still see people on the streets who look like Divine in costume.

IVES: When did you start making budgets?

WATERS: I still never make them. Rachel does. In the old days, I would say, "Okay, we're going to get this amount of money," and we made it work for whatever we got. Bob Maier helped me do that budget stuff for *Desperate Living* and *Polyester*.

IVES: There must have been priorities for where the money went. You had such a small amount, somehow you had to figure...

Divine and Tab Hunter made an unlikely pair in Polyester.

WATERS: I used to figure out how much it cost a day for all of the equipment, and then I would double it. If you look back on my old expense book for *Eat Your Makeup*, it says, "seventeen cents—shoes." It's the most pitiful expenses list.

IVES: But you could find that stuff then.

WATERS: I know. But it's shocking to look back how cheaply we did this stuff. I never saw one of those budget sheets—the kind we do now—until *Polyester*. I just somehow took whatever amount of money I had and made it work. Basically, I still do that. They ask for a budget and you figure, "Well, how much are they going to give me?" Then you make the budget for that amount.

IVES: Are your budgets less tight now than they used to be?

WATERS: *Cry-Baby* was certainly tight. I had a lip-synch coach, I had things that I have never had before. And *Cry-Baby* was hard to make on that amount of money. I've never felt like I've had money to burn. I want the people who give me money to make money. If my movies cost fifty million dollars,

I never trust filmmakers who say they don't care about their films making money.

they're never going to make any money. If they don't make money, I won't get to make the next one. That's the oldest rule there is. I never trust filmmakers who say they don't care about their films making money. Who's going to give them money to make the next one, then?

IVES: Somehow, there are certain filmmakers...

WATERS: ...who fail upwards. That's very possible in Hollywood. I don't want to name names, but I can think of a few. But how do they get the budget? Each one they make is a notorious failure, for a huge amount of money.... It amazes me. They must give a good pitch.

IVES: When you started, did you do second takes of things?

WATERS: Yeah, if it didn't work. In *Pink Flamingos*, I think we did. In *Multiple Maniacs*, we did. With Edith, we'd have to do fifteen takes. Edith was a film-eater.

IVES: She'd flub her lines or forget them?

WATERS: Yeah, like thirty takes. Twenty-five takes with the same mistake every time. And I'd just leave it in if it worked. She'd get flustered.

IVES: What kind of ratio did you have then?

WATERS: Oh, I've never known the answer to that question... I usually get it on, I would say, three takes. It depends on whether we're rushed, but I don't do a million takes. I think it gets worse. I mean, if you flub it up or there's a technical mistake like a dolly bump—that's what makes me do most takes over. But generally, after three or four takes, I don't think the performance gets better.

IVES: You don't try different interpretations?

WATERS: Once in a while, two. Just for a cushion. But I think the most we had in *Cry-Baby* was maybe eleven or twelve takes, and that was probably because of technical stuff, complicated camera work—not because of a performance.

IVES: Are you very involved with the editing process?

WATERS: Yeah. Well, I used to edit them.

IVES: When did you start having editors?

WATERS: On *Female Trouble* I had an editor named Charles Roggero, [the editor through *Polyester*] who did edit the movie—and I sat with him every single day all day. Same with *Desperate Living*. And *Polyester*. Janice Hampton did *Hairspray* and *Cry-Baby*; with her, I don't sit there at all. She does a rough assemblage in the beginning. Then I look at it, and we go through and make all the notes: "I like this, this, this and this...." Then I go away for three weeks, she does the stuff, and I come back and look at it. I say, "Well, try this, try this..." Then I go away until she does it; then she calls me and says, "Okay, come look at it." And that's fine; I don't want to be sitting there looking over her shoulder. You know, editors had to wean all that stuff away from me. In the beginning, I just did it myself. And it was hard to edit—there weren't a lot of choices in *Pink Flamingos* because of the single system. The choices were: "Do I cut this out or not?" There were only one or two takes. A lot of times there was just one long take of a scene, like a play.

IVES: Right. With no coverage.

WATERS: Because of the sound problem.

IVES: Do you still try to edit in your head while you're shooting?

WATERS: Oh, yeah. I always do that. I'm always thinking of the continuity. Will this match? Will this cut right? I'm paranoid about that, which you should be.

IVES: Was it hard to wean you away from the editing just because you were used to doing it yourself, or was it because you didn't want to let it go?

WATERS: I didn't know any other way. I hated filming them, actually. I mean, I didn't hate them, but I'm not mechanical. I've always been an actor's director. I'm not some technique person who knows every single thing about lighting. I want people to help, to tell me. I want to hire somebody who has that as their obsession. But in the old days, I guess that was the only way I knew.

IVES: Do you have a longer-than-usual editing process?

WATERS: I don't think so. With *Cry-Baby* it seemed like forever because of all the testing they do. They test it and then you've got to go try it, then test it again to see if that worked. That makes it longer, just because of how long it takes to show it, get the results, listen to the notes, go back—that kind of thing.

IVES: Do you think that's a good system?

WATERS: The first two tests are good, and after that it isn't good. We changed some things in *Cry-Baby*, and I have no idea today if it helped or hurt. There's a certain luxury to it in a way, though. Never before had I had the chance to see something that didn't work in one of my films and go back and change it. But I don't know that you can fine tune it like a car, which is what they really want—to control everything. I don't know if that's possible. If it were, every movie would be a hit.

IVES: How well do your films do?

WATERS: *Cry-Baby* hasn't made money. *Hairspray* will. And all the other films eventually made money, including *Desperate Living*, which took a long time.

IVES: Are the video releases working?

WATERS: Yeah, video helps. I don't know what happens after every foreign sale, every foreign video deal, every foreign theatrical deal and everything comes through. In the long run, maybe *Cry-Baby* will reflect that. But on paper, it lost money. And all the other ones will make money, but we're not talking *E.T.* here. We are talking steady income, though. I still get money from movies from twenty, twenty-two years ago. But I made more for writing and directing *Cry-Baby* than for all the other movies together.

IVES: Well, I would think so.

WATERS: But I like to think that twenty years' work is why I made that amount. If I were a first director coming in, I wouldn't have made that amount of money.

IVES: But it was also because *Cry-Baby* was a reasonably big-budget studio film.

WATERS: It made money for people, you know, for the movie theaters. And it did well in Europe. Plus I think it did something like a hundred and twenty thousand cassettes, first thing. That's not bad.

IVES: How long have you had an agent?

WATERS: Since right after *Hairspray*, came out. But, Bill Block, who is my agent, tried to help me to get the money for *Flamingos Forever* before that. Nobody would ever give me the money. He didn't give up though, he tried for a long time, for no money. He didn't get a penny for himself. Then he became quite successful with his own agency [Intertalent], and I remembered that he hadn't given up, so I called him after *Hairspray,* and he said he was just going to call me. So we hooked up then and he got me the *Cry-Baby* deal.

IVES: How does that relationship work?

WATERS: Fine. I mean, I went out there and said, "Okay this is the movie I want to make," and he said, "Okay." Then he set up all the meetings, and I went to them all, then he got me the deal. And my lawyer, Tom Hansen is part of the package. They both go in and do it. They're great.

IVES: Do you think all of that affects your work at all?

WATERS: Yes. It certainly gets me more money than I ever had before.

IVES: How has the process of planning, organizing and financing your films changed over the years?

WATERS: The major thing is that I don't have to go out and raise the money, which I really hated. It was really hard. I did that for all of them up to *Polyester*. I had to go pitch the idea and then ask all these people for twenty thousand dollars each.

IVES: Some of your films were put together that way?

WATERS: Yeah. *Female Trouble* was. *Desperate Living* was. In the early days I borrowed it from my father. Then I'd pay him back and say, "Can I double it?"

IVES: He doesn't invest in your movies now?

WATERS: No one does. I wouldn't want to ask him now, anyway. Back then, he did it. And he was so shocked that I paid him back, I think, that he told me with *Pink Flamingos*, "Don't pay me back. You're set up now. Keep that money. That's yours." It was great, like a fortune. Ten thousand dollars to me then was an eight-million-dollar budget to me now.

IVES: You've always been unusually involved in the business end of things, for a director.

WATERS: No, I hate doing the budgets. That's why I'm so glad for Rachel; she's so good at that. I only did it then because I had to— who else was going to do it?

IVES: So you don't like that aspect?

WATERS: I hate to talk with people about money. I mean, I *can* do it, and I'm not going to get screwed—I don't hate it that much. I read every

Pat Moran still uses open calls to get the Baltimore extras that help give Waters's films their unique texture.

word of my contract and ask my lawyer lots of questions.... And I sign every check. I don't hire somebody to do that kind of stuff; I know what I have and what's going on with it. But the part I'm so glad I don't have to do anymore is the producing stuff—all the money stuff and making deals with people. I hated that, especially when they were my friends.

IVES: You did that, Pat didn't do it?

WATERS: No, I did the money part of it. Pat eased other kinds of problems. She has a power on the set that's very hard to describe. When you come to

> *I sign every check. I don't hire people to do that. I know what I have, and I know what's going on with it.*

work on my movies, you have to make friends with her. It's the test. And most of them are very close with her, but she has a certain psychological power over the people we work with. With me also.

IVES: Do you feel good about that?

WATERS: Oh, yes. She's very valuable on a movie.

IVES: And you want that to continue?

WATERS: I want that. She knows the stuff that I don't like to do and she does that.

IVES: She said that she can't imagine you making a movie unless she was involved.

WATERS: No, I can't either.

IVES: And then I asked her, why she doesn't be the producer.

WATERS: Because budgets and equipment was never what Pat did for me. She always did casting, troubleshooting, in the old days script supervising, a million other jobs. She's a psychological producer. It's a new credit.

IVES: She's sort of like your right arm?

WATERS: Yes, completely. Or more like my right brain, my medulla. My support system.

IVES: Do you enjoy the production process? Do you enjoy shooting a film?

WATERS: In hindsight. I enjoy all of it afterwards, but it's torture when you're doing it. It's long, and it seems like it's never going to be over, and the hours, and the heat, and the anxiety—all that. I hate location scouting and ADR [additional dialogue recording]. Those are the two things I hate most out of the whole process. But it's better than having to get a real job.

IVES: Do you enjoy it less than you did before?

WATERS: No. I enjoy it the same, I think, but it's work. Never do I get up and go, "YIPPEE!" Sometimes I do feel that, though. I'm amazed when I get there and somehow all of these people are employed just because I have these ideas that might work. I pull up and see trucks and I think, "Teamsters actually have a job because of me?" That irony certainly makes me chuckle—that teamsters are treating me like the boss. There's a certain mind-boggling element to that. I enjoy it, but it's a huge relief when it's over. You're just so exhausted. The only reason everybody works that hard is because there's an end in sight. No one could work like that all the time, but I guess some crew people do. I have never understood how they could possibly do that.

IVES: They do, though.

WATERS: I know. But they don't have all the anxiety of dealing with the powers that be; they just go from one job to another. Whether it's a hit doesn't affect whether they get hired.

IVES: It almost doesn't matter what the film is, for most of them. It's a technical job.

WATERS: Yeah, but they get into it with the same obsession that I do, and I respect that. They love movies in the same way, or they wouldn't haven't chosen this career. What they do is different, but they have the same obsession about it. They like the gypsyism of it. They like the war aspect of it, that you pull into a neighborhood and tell people to move their cars, and they do. (Laughs.) I never quite understood why. You knock on doors and say, "You have to move your car, we're making a movie," and people say, "Oh, okay," and come out in their bathrobes and stuff. That's amazing to me. That makes it a good, special business. It's like the magic show's in town. The circus is here. And with my movies, it *is*—literally.

IVES: A truism about creative people and the creative process is that the ones who really take chances in life—who aren't afraid to leap without knowing what's going to happen—are the ones who achieve greatness.

WATERS: It's true even with Hollywood movies. Completely. A "no" is free. That's the only advice I ever give. Don't be afraid of people telling you no. Ask everything. You throw enough shit on the wall, something sticks; that's another old slogan I firmly believe in. Everybody's afraid of rejection. I think show business probably has the most insecure people—including me. That's why you choose that field, so the rest of the world can tell you you're good. And you've got to know that a lot of times people are going to say no to you, and that can't stop you. I went through six years when nobody would give me the money to make a movie. I didn't go happily walking around saying "Oh, gee..." It pissed me off and it depressed me, but I didn't give up. You have to take chances. And all of the Hollywood movies that say, "All right, this movie was a hit, let's make one like it," never work. The ones that do work aren't like other ones. That's why they work. But what young kids have to do, and I tell them this in school: A) You should always have sex

Always put sex and violence in your first movie. Even if it's bad, at least somebody will want to watch it.

and violence in your first movie, because even if it's bad, at least somebody will want to watch it; and B) Don't make a film about your grandmother. Don't make it so personal that no one but you cares about it. Somebody has to want to see it.

IVES: It's got to be on the edge somehow or some way.

WATERS: The first time, yeah. And you can't say, "Well, I don't care whether other people see it." Then why do you go to the trouble to make a movie? You want people to see it; that's the whole point, to get as many people as you can to come look at what you've done. So you have to do exactly what you want, but think of a fake way to make people think it will make money, know what I mean? At least attempt to give it a form so that people who know nothing about it will pay money to see it. You have to give the audience something they want. And I don't think that's selling out, I think it's selling *in* so that you can do what you want.

IVES: But I suppose that's something people wrestle with—the balance between doing what you want to do and being commercial.

WATERS: Yes. You have to think of a creative way to be commercial. Whatever your style is, you have to think of it commercially.

IVES: I was working with David Burton Morris, who did *Patti Rocks*. It was an interesting film with difficult subject matter, but he wanted to do it in black-and-white. And I talked him out of it, because I thought that it...

WATERS: ...it would be hard enough...

IVES: ...so why do it in a way that movie theaters won't play it?

WATERS: Exactly. But, you see, the other thing is that to be any kind of success in any kind of creative thing—writing, painting, anything—you have to be obsessed with it. And you can't fake that. You have to care about that more than ever, and you can't ever think it isn't going to happen. You can't be a filmmaker because you think it would be cool or you want to be famous. There are so many people now who just want to be famous; they don't want to do any work.

IVES: Or they do it because they want to make money.

WATERS: I think they want to be famous more than make money. But they don't want to do any of the things that you have to do. Because they think fame brings you something—and it doesn't. I mean, they think fame will answer every one of their problems, but it just makes the problems weirder. (Laughs.)

IVES: Is there anything that you think ought to be said that hasn't been said, information that you would like to impart about the process of filmmaking?

WATERS: The process of it has changed. I've gone through the process—it's different each time—of physically getting the money to make a movie. It's very different for me now than it used to be. When it's not through the studio system, you have to raise your own money, which all filmmakers have to do in the beginning.... You have to learn how to raise money.... You have to be a salesman. You have to be a grifter, almost. It's a thin line. Like selling the Brooklyn Bridge. Art dealers are good at that. But I guess at some point you have to find a certain type of rich person you can get along with. You can't hate the rich. Or, I guess you can, but it would really make your life miserable as a filmmaker because the world [of film] is controlled by the rich, and it costs a lot of money to make movies. So you can't have a chip on your shoulder about the rich.

> *You have to learn how to raise money. You have to be a salesman. You have to be a grifter, almost.*

IVES: You never hated the rich. You were making fun of them, but you didn't hate them.

WATERS: Well, it depends. Some of them I hated. It depended on what they were like. I didn't think rich always equals evil, because I had to go and get this money from these people. You've got to figure a way to do that. And that's something they don't ever teach you about. How to form a limited partnership. All that stuff. All those horrible things I used to have to learn. (Laughs.) I don't

understand why film schools don't make all their students read
the trade papers every day. I don't understand why they don't tell
them how to pitch. Maybe they do in L.A.

IVES: Well, UCLA has special seminars on production, producers,
lawyers, public relations....

WATERS: But in many film schools, I get the feeling that the attitude is
basically that if your films make money, they're bad films. I'm very
much against that. If I had kids and I was sending them to film school,
I'd be pissed. You know, that commercial cinema is bad, by definition.

IVES: Well, I think there are two schools of thought. It's almost like the
East Coast and the West Coast. In California, everybody wants to
get discovered by the...

WATERS: ...by the studios.

IVES: Yeah. At UCLA and USC, they have screenings of student films,
and there's competition as to who gets their films into the screenings, who gets to be the director on the films, or whatever. And then
they have big screenings.

WATERS: But that's wrong, too, because they have no idea what it's like
to make independent movies. I mean, they don't know what it's like
to go out there and make a film by hook or crook. I guess they do,
if they make them in school. But then I guess their parents pay for
them. Well, my parents paid for mine, so what can I say? But they
didn't have to figure some way for the films to get the money back.
That's what isn't taught.

IVES: Do you see yourself as being related to any classification of filmmaking?

WATERS: No, I think if anything I started my own genre that I've kept,
and maybe I'm the only person in it. When people think of me—
fortunately or unfortunately—they think "weird." They think weird
subject, weird film, that kind of thing. But I think basically the film
industry respects me enough to let me keep doing what I've been
doing all this time. I've stayed true to it, and that's what I do. And
I feel lucky about that.

IVES: What, to you, is the most important element that goes into a film?

WATERS: The subject, that's the most important. With each one of my
movies, you can see in almost every word what it's praising or what
it's attacking. And the subject has to fascinate me, or be what I'm
thinking about lately or what makes me laugh, in order to ever get
other people to share that laughter or obsession.

IVES: That's an interesting answer....

WATERS: What do you think most directors would answer?

IVES: Well, they would say, you know, the plot or the arc of the characters.

WATERS: No, it's the world. The world I'm going to take you into.

IVES: But in a sense you're unusual, in that you're a showman.

WATERS: That's the only way I could do it.

IVES: I mean, I meet people who write screenplays and who are directors, or want to be directors.

WATERS: But do they have a stand-up act?

IVES: Right, they don't.

WATERS: That's what I always open my stand-up act with: "Next time you plunk down your six bucks to go to a movie, ask yourself, does Stanley Kubrick do a stand-up act? I doubt it! Don't pay!" (Laughs.) I mean, I certainly don't think every director should have a stand-up act. I'm just saying it's a way I use to hopefully keep making movies.

Next time you plunk down your six bucks to see a movie, ask yourself, does Stanley Kubrick do a stand-up act?

IVES: So what's in the future?

WATERS: I hope just make a movie every couple of years, and write a book every once in a while. That's plenty. It's enough. I don't want any more than that.

IVES: How do you see yourself as an old man?

WATERS: Walking around this garden, with a nurse. (Laughs.)

IVES: A nurse in a bouffant hairdo.

WATERS: (Laughs.) Right. I don't know, I hope that I get to be an old man, I guess. I know so many people who have died, that it seems to me like quite a luxury to get to be an old man. But then, unfortunately, when you're an old man you have all these horrible things happen to you that don't happen when you die young, you know? It seems it should be reversed to me, that babies should have all the problems of old age, because they don't know any better and they just got here and you have to pay your dues. Once you've paid them, you should live carefree, and have better health. I think it's unfairly set up. And I never understood why people are more upset when a baby dies than an old man, because an old man has so many things he won't be able to do again, where a baby doesn't even know what to do yet. You know what I'm saying? The baby doesn't know yet the

The barf bag used to promote Pink Flamingos.

thrills of a Fassbinder movie. (Both laugh.) But an old man will lose that memory.

IVES: Well, your mind gets better, up to a point.

WATERS: Then it gets worse.

IVES: It all sort of falls apart at the end.

WATERS: The final indignity. Diapers. (Lets out a deep sigh.)

PARALLELS

PATTY HEARST • RACHEL TALALAY •
PIA ZADORA • RICKI LAKE •
SARA RISHER • PAT MORAN

Patty Hearst had a featured cameo role in *Cry-Baby*.

JOHN IVES: When did you first meet John Waters?

PATTY HEARST: I met him at the Cannes Film Festival, when the Patty
Hearst movie came out. [*Patty Hearst, written and directed by Paul
Schrader, recounts the publishing heiress's ordeal with the Symbionese
Liberation Army.*] John came running up, saying, "I thought you were
completely guilty before I saw this movie." I thought, "Oh, it's nice
to meet you, too." (Laughs.) He said, "I was at your trial, and I
remember when they brought in the birthday cake."

IVES: He had all those details.

HEARST: Yes, and he really has such a nice way of saying it all. It doesn't
sound like, "I remember when you stabbed your mother to death," or
something like that. He was really funny, because he was just so *into*
it. He's obviously deranged. (Laughs.) But harmless—and really nice.

IVES: But you knew who he was?

HEARST: Yes, I did. That helped. Otherwise I probably would have been
frightened.

IVES: At least he had some legitimacy because he was a film director—
although if you had seen all the films, you may not have thought so.

HEARST: Then I really *would* have been frightened. (Laughs.) Then he
said, "Oh, I wanted you to be in my movie." He had just made
Hairspray. It was certainly flattering, but I thought it was just some-

thing nice to say. Then a year later, he called and said, "I'm making another movie; do you want to be in it?"

IVES: Did you do rehearsals after you agreed to do it?

HEARST: Yes. I got a message that he wanted to see me; he had sent over a script and I had read through it once. So I went over to see him and we were talking and then he said, "Can you read for me?" That was *not* what I had counted on; nobody had said anything about this being an audition. I just said, "Yeah, I can *read*," and I gave a horrible reading. It was so bad, it was unbelievable. A couple of days later, though, they called and said John wanted me to be in it, but I had to come down [to Baltimore] early to rehearse. After a few minutes of rehearsal, John jumped up and ran over and hugged me and said, "Oh, I *knew* you could do it! Your audition was so awful, we had to bring you down here just to be sure." (Laughs.)

IVES: Were you familiar with John's earlier films when you met him?

HEARST: I had heard about *Pink Flamingos*—I don't think there's anyone who hadn't, if they went to college in the seventies—but I had not seen it.

IVES: Have you seen them now?

HEARST: Yes. When he interviewed me to do *Cry-Baby,* he asked me if I had seen them, and I said no, and he said, "Well, don't see them now! Please wait until after we do this movie." So I waited until afterwards, then I saw it [*Pink Flamingos*] and, of course, I burst out laughing. It wouldn't have scared me off. I thought it was funny that he seemed a bit sensitive about it.

IVES: So you didn't have any resistance to doing a movie with him?

HEARST: No, are you kidding? I mean, I'd like you to find someone who would say, "Oh no, I don't want to be in a movie." Anyway, I knew that something horrible wasn't going to go up on the screen, with people looking at it and saying, "Whoa! Peee-ew!" because if it were that bad, they'd just fire you. In fact, I was right—that's why they brought me down early. (Laughs.)

IVES: Was it fun?

HEARST: Yes, it was the most fun I've ever had. It was absolutely a gas. I highly recommend it to anyone who wants to drop out of school and work. It was the most fun in the whole world.

IVES: What was it like on the set?

HEARST: It was fun because John picks people he likes; I didn't see anyone not getting along with anyone else. In fact, while we were filming I

commented on that, and David Nelson said, "Well, this is really unusual. Normally everybody is mad at everybody else, and there is this feeling that something is really wrong, but you don't know what it is—you
can't wait to get out of there. This is an unusually happy group." I had
Mink [Stole] as a roommate, and she was really fun, although she and
Susan Tyrrell were going to fill up my garbage can with beer cans and
cigarette butts and call the *National Enquirer* to come and take photographs of my dissipation. (Laughs.) And seeing Polly [Bergen] was
fun, too. I know her from New York. When we did the courtroom
scene, she came in and was looking all around, so I said hello to her,
and she said hello, then she looked again and said, "Oh my God, I
didn't recognize you!" John had done his uglifying act on all of us.

IVES: That was actually Van Smith, right?

HEARST: Well, yes, but it really is the combined vision of both of them,
dragging everyone into the make-up trailer and costuming to make
us look our worst. (Laughs.)

IVES: What was John like during the filming? Was he demanding?

HEARST: No, but he knows what he wants, and if you're not doing it, he
will literally say, "I want you to move like this," and get down on the
floor and do some kind of a crawl. To the kids, he'd say, "I want you
to make a face like *this*," and he'd make a really funny face. Then he'd
make them practice it for him. He made it really easy. He was like that
with everybody. And he always insists that we say our lines to the people who are on-camera, even when we are off-camera ourselves, on the
theory that it helps the person on-camera say their lines better.

IVES: Because they are actually involved in a dialogue?

HEARST: Yes, instead of having a production assistant just reading the lines
off-camera. I got the impression that that isn't always done. I thought
it was fun to do all of that. I didn't go running back to my trailer when
I was finished with a scene. In fact, I didn't notice anybody doing that.
Most of the time, we pulled up chairs and sat around and talked. Pat
[Moran] was there, and we talked with her. That was when we had
our conversation about who had been either arrested, in rehab, or
under psychiatric care. We did a little survey of everyone. There were
a couple of triple-headers! (Laughs.) One girl came walking along—I
don't want to say who it was, because she was really upset by it—and
John said, "Hey, you ever been arrested?" and she said, "Yeah!" And
then, all of a sudden, she was in tears, because it had come out of her
mouth before she realized what she was saying. John had to take her

aside and tell her it was all right, you know: "Are you kidding? Get fired from *this* set? Who do you think is working here?"

IVES: But you were comfortable with all of that?

HEARST: Well, of course, they all knew *I* had been arrested.

IVES: You never felt exploited, or that anyone was stepping over the bounds?

HEARST: No, no.

IVES: John had a reputation as the Sleaze King; do you think he has more depth than that? I mean, do you think of him as an artist?

HEARST: There's definitely more depth than that, although he does love the sleaze. I think there will always be an element of sleaze and shock value to everything he does. In the scene [in *Cry-Baby*] where she [Traci Lords] swallows Cry-Baby's tears, that's just a glass of water with "TEARS" written on it, but it had everybody gagging. He doesn't have to have Divine bending down to eat a pile of fresh dog feces to get a gag response. (Laughs.) He can get it from something much more benign. What John does is definitely art.

IVES: Do you consider him to be a friend?

HEARST: Yes, I talk to him regularly. He has become a very good friend. We have taken him with us on vacation in California. We actually got him to go down a river on an inner-tube and to take some hikes with us. I think that's the most athletic activity he's ever done in his life. (Laughs.)

Patty Hearst (shown with David Nelson) made her unlikely acting debut in Cry-Baby.

RACHEL TALALAY

Rachel Talalay began as a production assistant on *Polyester,* which launched her on a career as producer of several *Nightmare On Elm Street* films and director of the last entry in the series. She produced *Hairspray* and *Cry-Baby* and seems destined to continue to play that role for Waters. She lives in Los Angeles.

JOHN IVES: How does John Waters work on the set?

RACHEL TALALAY: What makes John different from most other directors is that he is first a story and character director, then he's a technical director. He tends to write big scenes with twenty characters and, because we still have budget limitations, he has to figure out how he can get all of those characters on the screen in a limited amount of time. He's never really had the luxury of taking several days to shoot one scene. His priority is to carefully block the scene around his vision of chaos, not around making sure that a particular person ends up in a particular spot so that a crane shot will work in a certain way. And the way he directs actors is different from anyone I've worked with, because he can use anything—he can use a stick on the ground—to explain his point. I saw him work with Johnny Depp in the fight scene in *Cry-Baby;* he wanted Johnny to be really heroic, so instead of just telling him that he wanted him to be like Errol Flynn or something, he ran up and sang "Ride of the Valkyries" to him. Johnny just looked at him [in surprise] and the next thing we knew, Johnny was this hero coming down the hill. That was a remarkable John Waters moment. Afterwards, Johnny had a glow on his face and he said, "That's the only time I've been directed like *that!*"

IVES: So John makes it clear what he wants from each actor.

TALALAY: He could play every character, exactly. He doesn't do that anymore, but he could. That's what he's drawing on. He draws very strongly on music as well. The scenes are written around songs and you can tell that's always in his mind when he directs. Most people add the music later, but I have sat with John while he has actually sung the song he's going to use—during an establishing shot—to figure out how far he wants the actual shot to go.

IVES: Does he use storyboards?

TALALAY: He wouldn't if I didn't ask him to. He has it all in his head. But in order to schedule some of the more complex special effects, I asked him to do some storyboards—like for the chicken race at the end of *Cry-Baby*—and he did. For some directors, story boards are the key to the whole movie, but John is different.

IVES: Does he stick to the script?

TALALAY: Oh, yeah. He doesn't whip out a script then run around improvising. And he hates it when actors do that, even in a reading. He wrote those words because he sat down and thought about every single one of them. That is an important distinction with him. It's not as though he's rigid, but he is very serious about the writing process.

IVES: Does he do a lot of takes?

TALALAY: No. We were probably under-budget on film for *Cry-Baby*. He's not excessive in any way. He's very careful and smart about that.

IVES: Does he keep track of the amount he's spending as he goes along?

TALALAY: I've had to teach him not to do that. He doesn't have to anymore. I do that for him now, and unless I say something, there's no problem. He can read me like a book. During *Cry-Baby*, I would walk on the set with a certain look on my face, and his favorite line was: "What fresh hell is this?"

IVES: He knows that the movie has to make money.

TALALAY: First of all, he has more integrity than anyone I know. And he's tremendously honest and caring. You know, people who don't know him [who have seen his earlier movies] think he must be some kind of monster, but he's nothing like that. He's so non-threatening and non-judgmental, people want to confide in him. And, of course, he has that tremendous sense of humor. He's real-

Sonny Bono (shown with Debbie Harry) played an ambitious amusement park owner in Hairspray, the first movie Rachel Talalay produced for Waters.

ly remarkable. He has such a comfortable way with himself, that he immediately makes other people relax.

IVES: Does he get uptight when he watches the dailies?

TALALAY: He gets uptight all the time. That's the other side of him. He worries about every detail. We all do.

IVES: What is his involvement with the editing process?

TALALAY: Complete. Until *Hairspray*, he had always edited the film with the editor. He was physically present, practically making the splices. On *Hairspray*, I told him we didn't have time for that, that the editor would edit the film and he would look at their assembly. He said, "How do they know what I want?" So I told him that a good editor would know from the way he shot it, and that he could talk to the editor about it. John was used to doing it all himself. It was a terrifying process for him to even let them put their hands on the film without him being in the room. But I hired a really good editor [Janice Hampton] whom he now can't live without. At first, it was very difficult for him, but now he doesn't even want to sit in the editing room.

IVES: Does he argue with her [Hampton] about what she's done?

TALALAY: No. First of all, John is not an arguer. And secondly, it is always his vision; everyone is respectful of that. And he does everything with such humor. Even if he doesn't like something, he finds something hysterical to say about it. He lets everybody talk about it. He is not afraid of that. The whole thing is an open process, but it is absolutely his decision.

IVES: Has he been helpful to you in terms of your own directing?

TALALAY: Sure. Watching his ability with people is incredibly helpful. It's funny; when people who like him find out that I'm his producer, it automatically makes me okay with them. I know that helped me get some of the cast for *Nightmare on Elm Street*. It definitely helped me get Rosanne Barr [Arnold]. I don't know if John even realizes how much he has helped me. He also helps by being a friend; he knows what I'm going through.

PIA ZADORA

Pia Zadora, movie actress, successful singer and recording artist, had a memorable cameo in *Hairspray.*

JOHN IVES: How did you end up playing a beatnik in *Hairspray?*

PIA ZADORA: He wanted me to play the prom queen but I was on tour. I didn't really want to play the prom queen, anyway; I wanted to do something a little more mature and sophisticated. So I said, "I'd love to, but I can't because I'm on tour." But I happened to have one free day between Philadelphia and Washington, so John asked me if I would do a cameo. So I said I'd love to, and I asked him what I'd be doing and if he wanted me to bring anything—hair, makeup, whatever. He said, "No, just come. Don't worry about a thing. Everything's going to be great." Of course, John is the only person in the world I would ever do that for—because I love him, because I trust him, because he's great. When it comes to John, you just do it, no matter what. I have blind faith in him. So I went down, and he said, "Okay, you're going to be a beatnik." And I said, "A beatnik? John, I was a very sheltered, shy little girl from Queens. My mother never let me get close to one." He just said, "Don't worry, you're going to *be* one." So he got me the bongos, handed me *Howl* [Allen Ginsberg's epic poem], I was singing "Day-O" [the "Banana Boat Song"], I had on the black wig and the white make-up, and he said, "Don't worry, you'll get out there and become the person." I was scared to death. I was a fish out of water. But the atmosphere on that set was so relaxed, he was like a father to all of these people. He was so nurturing, it wasn't even like a set. There wasn't that tension that normally exists. And it went from the lowest member of the crew to Ricki [Lake]; everybody was just out there to have a good time. There was no pressure. There was a parental kind of control in that everything was moving along and he was getting everything going, but in a very relaxed fashion. He made it so easy that by the time I knew what was going on, it was over. He just led everybody through it in a strong, yet gentle manner. I have never seen that kind of an atmosphere on a set before.

IVES: Have you seen all of his movies?

ZADORA: When I first met him, I hadn't. I was very sheltered and I was never really into his films until I met him and hooked into the person. *Hairspray* really had nothing to do with that [his earlier films]. It was a straightforward, PG-rated, funny film.

IVES: With his touches.

ZADORA: Definitely, with him woven into it. That's what made it so interesting and so unique. His mind was in that film. And Divine was such a phenomenon. Then he died, and I don't think John will ever recover from that. It was such a loss for him, almost like losing a mate.

IVES: His talent hasn't waned at all, though.

ZADORA: He has been a little more reclusive since that happened, but he's developing and working.

IVES: Are you doing more movies?

ZADORA: No.

IVES: Would you want to work with John again?

ZADORA: Oh, I'd love to work with John. He is the exception to the rule. That's a labor of love. All of the people [who work with Waters] are like offspring of his thought. They almost think along his lines and execute what he thinks and believes. That's what so great about John. He has a kind of power over people—in a very comfortable way, not in an oppressive way. You get excited when you talk to him because he inspires confidence.

IVES: People want to confess to him.

ZADORA: Because he's so warm and open, and because he takes the time to listen. That's a very rare quality.

IVES: What do you think of him as a filmmaker?

ZADORA: I think he has a lot to say. The thing about John is that his sensibility is an intimate one, it's very special. He is really able to give of himself. He is able to put that little stamp on everything he does, on every scene, on every character.

IVES: Do you think that the big-production-number approach of *Cry-Baby* got away from that?

ZADORA: I like him better in an intimate environment where he can convey—in a very precise way—what he's about, or what he has to give to a character, or what he has to say about what's going on in the world. But everything he does is good, because he's so creative and he has such a great sense of humor. In my book, he can't go wrong. John is ageless and timeless. He's always going to be one of the great filmmakers because he's a survivor. He's always going to keep coming back with something important. John will die making films. He'll die on a set; it's his life.

Pia Zadora's "blind faith" in her friend Waters, resulted in her memorable beatnik cameo in Hairspray.

RICKI LAKE

Ricki Lake was a teen-aged singer and actor attending college when she was asked to read for the lead role in *Hairspray*. She has since appeared on television's *China Beach* and in several films, including *Last Exit to Brooklyn* and *Cry-Baby*. Waters has said he can't imagine making a film without her now.

JOHN IVES: Did you become friends with Divine during *Hairspray?*

RICKI LAKE: Afterwards, yes. But not during the [filming of the] movie. He sort of resented me, because he wanted to play both roles. Initially, he was willing to have a face lift in order to play the daughter and the mother. Then suddenly here was this fat girl coming in and taking over, taking center stage. He was a little wary of me. But when we finished the movie, he accepted me and gave me advice; he treated me like I was his daughter. His mother started calling me the granddaughter she never had. Then we did become friends and I started hanging out, socially, with him.

IVES: But not for very long.

LAKE: No, unfortunately. Just for a few months.

IVES: Did he teach you anything on the set?

LAKE: He taught me to walk in high heels.

Ricki Lake (left, with Johnny Depp and Traci Lords in Cry-Baby) first worked with Waters on Hairspray.

SARA RISHER

Sara Risher is president of the production division at New Line Cinema, the company that first released Waters's films and also produced *Polyester* and *Hairspray*.

SARA RISHER: John Waters was a complete underground sensation [when New Line started working with him]. Nobody "above ground" had ever heard of him. His cult status on *Pink Flamingos* had spread by word of mouth. *Female Trouble* brought him into the mainstream; the day after the opening, *New York* magazine ran a huge story in the movie section. The headline was: "Smutty Waters." It was the first legitimate review he had, and the press was just buzzing after that.

JOHN IVES: When *Female Trouble* came out, *Pink Flamingos* had only been out for a year. He [John Waters] said that New Line sat on *Pink Flamingos* for about a year [before releasing it].

RISHER: Bob Shaye [chairman and CEO of New Line] didn't really know what to do with it. John [Waters] was the one who got it in the midnight shows at the Elgin Theater. He worked a lot on his own on that; it was his idea to hand out flyers and all that. Bob had always liked *Pink Flamingos*—he followed John's sense of humor and appeciated his talent from the beginning—but he just wasn't sure what to do with it. We had been playing it in every college town in America, but it was still underground. It hadn't gotten any legitimate press attention at that point.

IVES: Somewhere around that time, you also started to release his earlier films—*Mondo Trasho* and *Multiple Maniacs*.

RISHER: Yes, we went back to them. And we were very involved in the production of *Desperate Living*. We didn't literally produce it, but we were involved from the beginning. *Polyester* was the first [of Waters's films] that we fully financed.

IVES: How closely was John involved with you in terms of distributing the films?

RISHER: Completely and totally. He is a hands-on person when it comes to publicity; he is a master at it. And he understands what sells. He was involved in the trailers, the ad campaigns, the pitches, how to get word-of-mouth going—all of the marketing. We have always felt that he knows best how to sell the films and who his audience is. We never had an argument with him over how to sell a film until *Polyester*. We had gone to a very expensive ad agency, and they came up with a one-sheet that had a big toilet and a picture of Divine; all of the scratch-and-sniff smells—pizza, shoes, and all that—were coming out of the toilet. John hated that ad, and he was right.

IVES: How did you come up with the smells?

RISHER: When John first came to us with the idea for *Polyester*, he had the idea to use scratch-and-sniff, and he knew he wanted Divine to play a housewife. So he spent a year writing the script, and I spent a year researching the smells. I spent an entire year of my life trying to get smells for farts, marijuana, stinky shoes, and all of the other ones. (Laughs.) I had to convince 3M [the company that produced scratch-and-sniff] that this was a wholesome, family movie. I couldn't tell them I wanted fart smells; I had to say I needed rotten eggs or something. We had to design the smell. And I couldn't tell them that the poor housewife was played by a transvestite. When we were finished with the movie, they came to New York to see it, and we never heard from them again. I'm sure they were mortified.

IVES: What was it like, working with John?

RISHER: John's cast and crew will do anything for him, even if they get fed peanut butter sandwiches. He inspires so much loyalty and commitment. He's a sweetheart, but he's very demanding and people want to please him.

IVES: He's a father figure.

RISHER: He has an extremely warm heart; he's a caring, loving person. But he also has the funniest sense of humor in the world. And he reads *everything*, the minute it comes out in print. He's phenomenally bright.

IVES: Have his films made money?

RISHER: They've certainly made their money back, or we wouldn't have kept making them. But *Hairspray* didn't make the kind of money it should have, given the publicity and all of the good reviews it got. It was so well-loved that we tried to broaden the market, from one or two theaters in each town to twenty in each town, but that bombed. It seemed to work for the John Waters audience, who are people with a quirky sense of humor, older people who read film reviews, people who grew up on *Pink Flamingos,* a gay audience, and college kids. But when it got to the average American, it didn't seem to work. It made money, but not a lot.

IVES: Did that have anything to do with why you didn't do *Cry-Baby*?

RISHER: We didn't do that for two reasons. One, John had paid his dues. He had worked so hard for so little money for so long, that when he had an opportunity with a big agent to make a lot of money, we all thought he should do it. Two, we felt the budget was too expensive. We loved the idea, but we felt the market was somewhat limited. We did make an offer for four or five million, but John wanted to spend more on it. Then Universal and Imagine came in and gave him what he wanted. I'm really pleased for him, and I think he should continue doing that—then after he's made all his money he should come back to New Line. (Laughs.) We'd certainly love to do something with him again.

IVES: Did you like his earlier films?

RISHER: Bob [Shaye] loved them, and it was one of the weirdest experiences of my life. I'm a Catholic girl; I went to convent schools. So I had the same kind of rebellious instincts that John had, but I repressed them. I was thinking, "My God, this is everything I would have liked to have said and done, but never had the nerve!" I have always loved them. *Polyester* and *Hairspray* are two of my favorite films we've ever done at New Line.

IVES: Were you friends with Divine?

RISHER: Sort of. I knew him, of course. He was a very sweet man.

IVES: Not at all like his earlier characters.

RISHER: Oh, not at *all*. And, of course, John is not at all like his movies, either. I had a terrible crush on him. I was *crazy* about him. Of course, I knew he wasn't interested in me, but he told me that I was the only woman his mother ever thought he should marry. You know, I was a nice Catholic girl and I was from Virginia—the right side of the tracks. I was everything he had run away from. (Laughs.) John, as a person, is accepted by everybody. Everybody—young, old, every walk of life, every color—adores John Waters. They like what he writes and they like *him*. But his films always seem to take that seventies approach to the world, and I think he's past that. He could broaden his base so much in terms of his film work, and he didn't do that in *Cry-Baby*. The reason *Hairspray* worked—and *Cry-Baby* didn't—was that he had a very vulnerable protagonist [played by Ricki Lake] in *Hairspray*, someone everybody could relate to and care about. In *Cry-Baby*, I don't think we felt for any of the characters in that same way. I would like to see him do something far broader that could reach more people; kids today need to see John Waters's films to stir them up. We begged him to do a sequel to *Hairspray*, about the late sixties. We offered him carte blanche, but he doesn't want to do it.

IVES: Do you think he is an artist?

RISHER: Oh, yes. He interprets life with his own special vision. As an artist, he defined a lot of the seventies and early eighties. Maybe he can do that for the nineties.

Waters on Divine: "He started his career playing a homocidal maniac and ended playing a loving mother—if that's not good acting, what is?"

PAT MORAN

Pat Moran is John Waters's closest friend. She lives in Baltimore and manages the Charles Theatre, the city's finest repertory movie house. Moran has been Waters's right-hand person on nearly every film he has made, as well as his confidante and one of the few people he uses as a sounding board when he is writing. She has also served as his casting director, with an exceptional talent for digging up the unusual local extras who give his movies an unmistakable Waters texture. On the set, Moran is a buffer, protecting Waters from problems and allowing him to concentrate on the creative aspects of directing.

PAT MORAN: John's greatest asset is his sense of humor. But the guy's a workaholic—work is his drug of choice. We talk to each other constantly on the phone—eight to ten times a day—and we both talk very fast. He calls, no matter where he is in the world, if I'm not with him. We have our own language that can speed it up, especially if it's on a dime in Munich or somewhere. We can get a lot done in three minutes.

JOHN IVES: How long have you been working together?

MORAN: Since the beginning. I've been in all of [Waters's films], but you have to look for me—there are a lot of disguises. I mean, it's not as though a Waters actress had to be qualified; we weren't Julie Harrises. But somewhere along the line I decided I didn't want to be up front. I wanted more longevity, even though I didn't really believe it [the filmmaking] would ever really come to anything. We had grown up with Hollywood movies and a few renegades. Then along came Warhol, and it showed us that there was another kind of movie that could be made. Then, of course, John went off to NYU for about twenty minutes. He had no intention of looking at Eisenstein films; he was down on Forty-second Street watching the Grind-o-rama and hideous films by every lunatic in the world.

IVES: Did you like that stuff, too?

MORAN: Not really. But I loved all the ludicrous Russ Meyer stuff because it was so stupid—and also, you could tell it cost a dollar to make. That's what we were about. We had no money. The most essential part of filmmaking is the money, let's get real about that. You can say anything you want, but if your money is not in place, you cannot complete your film. It was as intense for us to get two grand for *Mondo Trasho* as it was to get eight million to do *Cry-Baby*.

IVES: Rachel Talalay was the producer on *Cry-Baby*, where did she come from?

MORAN: She was a production assistant on *Polyester*. I rode her relentlessly, if you want the truth. But when she walked away from that, she said she learned everything. There were no women in film then; it was a man's world. We worked eighteen hours a day. I didn't want to see anybody sit down. I knew that if John could continue, we could continue. The most important thing when you're making a movie—besides getting the money—is the movie itself. Not Desert Storm. Not that you happen to have tonsillitis at the time.

IVES: Well, filmmaking is an obsessive art.

MORAN: Yeah, but I've worked a lot of big Hollywood movies—doing location casting when they come to Baltimore—and it's sometimes *not* [obsessive]. I've seen a different sensibility. We did our pick-up shots for *Cry-Baby* in Los Angeles and certainly that work ethic was not as prevalent there as it is here.

IVES: What do you see as John's strengths and weaknesses as a filmmaker?

MORAN: His strength is that he is relentless, nothing is impossible. He just gets it done. He has always lived his life by a file card. The file card says what has to be done, and if it's not completed, it gets carried over to the next day's file card. That's called file-card-ism. It's a major strength. I don't know what his weaknesses would be. Anything that could be described as a weakness is not on his agenda. Another strength is the way he treats people. First of all, he takes no nonsense. He is the director, period. But he's great to everybody—he never leaves without saying good-bye to people, he always treats people well. That's why people work for him—in a way that money can't buy.

IVES: People seem to fall in love with him.

MORAN: There's a certain magic on his set, no matter what the horror of the day is—it's raining and you're supposed to be outside, or the camera goes down, or any of the dilemmas of filmmaking. People are wild about him, and it's because he treats them decently. He's accessible, polite—even the Teamsters loved him.

IVES: He seems to develop lasting friendships with people who work with him.

MORAN: John is a very loyal person, and he also demands loyalty. He doesn't just tell you what you want to hear. So people respect him.

IVES: People have a difficult time accepting how straight you [and John Waters and the crew] are.

MORAN: Well, you get older and you get a little bit tired. But did people really think that Alfred Hitchcock was killing people in showers? Are they really that naive, to think that directors are really what their movies are?

IVES: Do you think of John as an artist?

MORAN: *No!*

IVES: Maybe artist is the wrong word.

MORAN: It *is* the wrong word.

IVES: Is he a great director, the way Scorsese is a great director?

MORAN: It's really hard to even say *that*. I imagine they direct their movies in the same way, the way they approach the details of the total picture—the costumes, the production design, *everything*. John makes comedies; it's a different story to make *Hairspray* as opposed to *Raging Bull*, or *Mean Streets* as opposed to *Pink Flamingos*.

IVES: Making a comedy is no less a serious expression of ideas.

MORAN: No, and no less intense. John is a writer/director. Scorsese is certainly involved in that; Levinson is, Woody Allen is. Writer/directors are a breed above the average director. And John worked against all odds with his stuff. The outrageousness was just comedy blown way out, like in *Pink Flamingos*. If you've only got twelve thousand dollars, what else are you going to do to get somebody to notice you?

IVES: It's not just trash and shock and outrageousness, though. There

John Waters refers to longtime friend and collaborator Pat Moran as "my right brain, my medulla."

are things that he's saying in those films.

MORAN: But he's never been a director who has gone out and said, "I have a message I'm going to give you"—even with *Hairspray*, which certainly said something. And I doubt if Scorsese does that, either. They're both storytellers; one tells jokes and the other one doesn't.

IVES: What do you look for when you're casting one of John's films?

MORAN: When I read one of his scripts, I know what it looks like, the same way a production or costume designer does. When you've been working with the same guy since he was seventeen, you ought to know something. So, I look for what defined the character in my mind—the way I saw them—the first time I read the script. I make suggestions as to who we might want to take a look at. And he has some ideas. We do it together, with the producer.

IVES: You have moved, to some extent, from the Dreamland Studios in-house crew to a wacko against-type celebrity cast technique.

MORAN: Oh yes, we like that because we never could do it before. If you had a real budget, wouldn't you like to work with somebody you always wanted to know about? Then if you call them in and they can't read a line, at least you got to see them.

IVES: You test them all?

MORAN: Sure. But with casting, they get on a level—this is Hollywood bullshit—where they're "meeting." You don't ask people to read.

IVES: When the bigger names come in for a "meeting," even though you can't ask them to read, do you test them out some way?

MORAN: We just talk to them and ask them a few questions. He tells them what it's about, and the smart ones offer to read. They're usually fairly amenable.

IVES: A lot of Hollywood casting is done, not by searching anywhere-and-everywhere for the best person to play the part, but by looking for a name that might fit. Do you ever look for a name?

MORAN: We never could before *Cry-Baby.* We didn't have the money. And that was the first one where we needed a youth star, so John looked at all the teen magazines, and he asked my daughter, who is that age. Johnny [Depp] turned out to be just like we are. He really wanted to do it, and he keeps in touch to this day.

IVES: Where do you see John—and you—going in terms of films?

MORAN: I don't know. If he could have it the way he wanted it, he'd make a movie every year. That would be great.

IVES: Why can't you do that?

MORAN: Well, first of all, it's a long process that doesn't allow for it [making a movie every year], especially if you're the kind of director who's in the editing room, listening to the music, checking how the credits look, doing everything. And *Cry-Baby* wasn't exactly a big hit in America. I mean, had that come in with money like *Star Wars*, we could have made one [the next] year. I really don't know where it's going to take us. No one could've ever told me, years ago, that I would be at Cannes; so it's really difficult to project where we're going. I just hope we can continue to make movies the way we want to make them.

IVES: Have you ever read a book or had some idea in your mind and said it would be a great movie to make?

MORAN: No, there was only one that we ever thought about, and that was *A Confederacy of Dunces*. But I'd like to see him do a really serious movie, probably a psychodrama. Something like *Silence of the Lambs*, because that's the one that scared people the most. I'd like to see how it would work. Maybe some of the comedic sense could be worked into it. I always wanted to see Divine do Sidney Greenstreet roles. He probably would have, had he lived. I think eventually he would have done something really great as a heavy. I know he could have pulled it off.

PROD. CRY-BABY

ROLL	SCENE	TAKE
233	46D	3

| DIRECTOR | J. WATERS | A |
| CAMERA | D. INSLEY | |

7·6·89   NITE   EXT   5296

TIMELINE

Filmography

1964

Hag in a Black Leather Jacket: Much of this 8-mm, black-and-white film was shot on the director's bewildered parents' roof. Like the next two, this seventeen-minute work was never released. However, several key Waters themes are already apparent, particularly the role of the tormented woman (here not so much tormented as trapped in a bizarre dream).

It is the story of a girl (Mona) who marries a black man in a rooftop ceremony performed by a Ku Klux Klansman. The film opens with Mona home alone, watching as the black man drives up with a garbage can in the front seat of his car. She drives off with him, changes into a ballet outfit as he watches, and then dances. The black man gets inside the garbage can, and she must load it into the car.

Meanwhile, the Klansman is perched on a chimney, seeming almost angelic. This could be Waters's first exploration on film of the sacred symbols of Catholicism. Various characters, including a girl with wild hair and a man in drag, also find themselves on the roof. Mona appears in a bridal gown, her train carried by a child. The black man emerges from the can, and everyone is on the roof eating wedding cake as the Klansman descends. At the end, Mary

Vivian Pearce dances the "bodie green," a sexy dance, as Waters's own mother plays "God Bless America" on the piano.

1966

Roman Candles: Actually three 8-mm films shown simultaneously (now recorded onto videotape divided into four quadrants, one always blank), this was shot in color and introduced several more Dreamland regulars, including David Lochary, Mink Stole, Pat Moran, and Divine. Also appearing was Maelcum Soul, who exerted an important influence on Divine and Van Smith in terms of style, particularly eye make-up.

Again, the images are wild and arty, and at first seem random. The film uses the multiple images to allow religion, bizarre lifestyles, and everyday life to play off each other, juxtaposed with split-second shots from old horror flicks.

Several scenes involve drug-taking or weird sex, both of which were used to emphasize both the absurd and the provocative in many of Waters's later, more accessible films. There are scenes of religious mockery, including Maelcum dressed as a nun. The woman-under-attack theme surfaces, as Mary Vivian Pearce is attacked with an electric fan, and a man in black leather beats another woman; later, Mona, dressed as a bride, whips one of the men.

The end of the film is a surprisingly poignant montage, under a nostalgic Shangri-Las tune. The sequence shows one actor photographing Mona, another in drag on a motorcycle, David Lochary firing a shotgun, Divine in a red wig, a shot of Lee Harvey Oswald's mother, and finally Divine playing hide-and-seek. While it may not sound particularly touching, the way Waters weaves together the images and music is tremendously effective.

1967

Eat Your Makeup: This black-and-white film was shot in 16-mm, and at forty-five minutes contains a fairly linear narrative. It follows an evil couple, played by David Lochary (in the first of several roles as a perverted gangster) and Maelcum Soul, who kidnap young women and chain them in the woods. When an audience gathers, they compel their prey to model themselves to death. The only food provided for the poor victims is platefuls of cheap make-up. The three captives (Marina Melin, Mary Vivian Pearce and

Mona Montgomery) grovel shamelessly for the nourishment. Beautiful women chained to a freestanding wall, then forced to flaunt themselves before a jeering crowd until they drop dead—all couched in the language of style and fashion—works as a powerful metaphor for our image-conscious, media-saturated society.

This is the first Waters film to explore the theme of the evil group that exploits others and revels in its own wickedness. In later films, this group inevitably loses; the misfits who are comfortable with their own deviance end up winning. Here, however, the bad guys triumph.

The black-and-white images are quite intense, despite the graininess of the crudely filmed production. Waters uses depth of field to create a beautiful and studied pacing. Two sequences, both figuring religion, are instantly memorable. As the opening credits roll, the wicked couple and a vicious dog on a chain stalk Marina (wearing a peekaboo dress) as she emerges from church fingering her rosary. Later, as a bishop intones the sacraments, Divine fantasizes while reading a magazine. We see Divine as Jackie Kennedy and Howard Gruber as JFK riding in an open car, waving to invisible crowds over sounds of cheering. As an aria builds, a shot is fired, Howard slumps over, and Divine—in a pillbox hat and bloodstained pink dress—climbs over the back of the car as it takes off. Laughter fills the screen as Divine fades back to reality.

After Marina dies on the runway and the wicked ones depart, a man in a cavalry uniform puts flowers on the body and kisses her. She comes back to life as a fairy princess and walks into the woods. This is another of Waters' recurring elements: the deformed fairy tale as metaphor for modern society.

1969

Mondo Trasho: Made in 16-mm black-and-white, this ninety-five-minute film was Waters's first to eventually find distribution, through New Line Cinema, although not until after *Pink Flamingos* became a hit in 1973. In some ways Waters's most poignant, sensitive film, it was shot entirely without dialogue, and is considered by Waters himself to be one of his most bizarre and difficult.

The film tells the story of a truly tormented woman, played by Mary Vivian Pearce, who goes on a terrible one-day adventure. As Pearce strolls through the park, she is accosted by a maniacal foot fetishist, who "shrimps" her (toe-licking) in the woods.

After the seduction, she wanders alone out of the park to a road, where she is run over by Divine in a Cadillac convertible with the radio blasting. In an effort to hide her crime, Divine takes the girl with her. She shoplifts clothes and shoes in a thrift shop, then lays the girl on a laundromat table and dresses her.

The Virgin Mary and an angel appear in the laundromat, granting Divine's prayer for help by materializing a wheelchair. Divine wheels the girl off. They are soon abducted and taken to an asylum reminiscent of *The Snake Pit*, inhabited by a topless dancer and various Fellini-esque characters. In the midst of this mayhem, the Virgin Mary again answers Divine's prayer by covering the prone girl with a fur coat and giving Divine a knife, which she uses to escape. Fascinatingly, the plot begins with disaster for the girl, but creates torment for them both, as Divine—now committed to caring for the girl, quite tenderly and protectively—is put through a series of terrible trials of her own. Divine, as in later films, is a mockery of a beauty queen/criminal, redeemed through a series of traumatic encounters with forces far more evil and threatening than she could ever be.

The story reaches its climax when Divine brings the girl to an insane doctor with magic powers, played by David Lochary, who amputates the girl's feet and replaces them with horribly misshapen monster feet. This repugnant act nonetheless brings the girl back to life, albeit in a trance (in a tantalizing reversal of Michael Powell's *The Red Shoes*).

Meanwhile, Divine, pursued by evildoers, dies in a muddy pigsty, to the sound of Wagner's "Ride of the Valkyries". The girl awakens among the grunting pigs and is in shock to discover her transmogrified feet. But the mad doctor has imbued her with magic powers of her own: by clicking her heels together, she can transport herself á la Dorothy in *The Wizard of Oz*. Praying and clicking, she finds herself in the downtown shopping district, where two older women disdainfully fire a volley of epithets at her: "Whore, B-girl, rimmer, slut" etc. She clicks her heels once again and disappears.

1969

The Diane Linkletter Story: Made about the same time as *Mondo Trasho*, this fifteen-minute, black-and-white film presages Divine as the youthful Dawn Davenport in *Female Trouble*. After Divine presents the opening credits while doing various drugs, the film begins with a voice-over of a letter from Diane (yet another tragic female) to her parents.

The parents (Mary Vivian Pearce and David Lochary!) are fretting over their daughter's wild behavior: taking drugs, and hanging out on the Strip [Sunset Boulevard] with her boyfriend.

Diane enters, wrecked on drugs, and responds to her parents' shocked concern, "I am what I am, doing my own thing in my own time." This was the slogan of the sixties, a period Waters ridiculed at every opportunity, despite his own at least vicarious involvement in some of the era's wilder excesses. Diane is on LSD, and her father calls a doctor. When Diane protests, her mother slaps her, and she runs to her room, crying bitterly. Her father yells up the stairs, calling his daughter a "disgusting slut."

In a drugged delirium, the teenager goes to the window, opens it, and falls out, screaming as she tumbles to the ground. Over a high shot of her bloody body, we hear the parents' final plea: "So please come back to us. We love you. Call collect."

1970

Multiple Maniacs: Made in 16-mm black-and-white, this was the first film to feature actual in-synch (if crudely recorded) dialogue. The ninety-minute film was later released by New Line Cinema and starred Divine, David Lochary, Mink Stole and Edith Massey.

It also provides the most insane and least sympathetic role in Divine's career; she begins and ends the film a hopeless homicidal criminal—even claiming to have murdered Roman Polanski's late wife Sharon Tate—with few redeeming moments in between. But the film, Waters's most overtly political, explores more vividly than ever the themes of the tortured outsider in a male-dominated society, the hypocrisy of religion—particularly Catholicism—gangs, sexual perversion, and the excesses of the sixties.

The film opens with Lady Divine's Cavalcade of Perversions, "the most flagrant violation of natural law ever known to man." Inside the tent are sideshows that make Tod Browning's *Freaks* look like the Easter Parade: the Bicycle Seat Sniffer, the Bra Sniffer, the Armpit Licker, the Puke Eater, a pile-up of writhing naked bodies, "actual queers kissing", and a heroin addict going "cold turkey." Divine sits in a separate area, attended by worshipping gang members. Once their curious marks have settled in, Divine and her gang emerge to rob and murder them.

The gang runs off. Later, Divine goes for a stroll downtown, a now-famous scene where she does her unparalleled-in-history, criminal-drag-queen-strut in a tight skirt, leopard top and spike heels. She is dragged into a doorway and raped by a woman, and a man in a dress and beard.

Recovering quickly, Divine is befriended by the Infant of Prague. The following sequence, clearly influenced by Bunuel's *Viridiana*, is perhaps Waters's most biting and outrageous attack on his Catholic roots. Inside the church, Divine kneels at a pew and prays. She is accosted by a lesbian, played by Mink Stole, who kisses her and proceeds to give her what Waters refers to as the "rosary job," penetrating her from behind with a rosary cross and bringing her to a wild orgasm. As if this were not enough, Waters reenacts the crucifixion of Christ, cutting shamelessly back and forth from the two lesbians cavorting in the church to the last supper, the betrayal of Jesus, the march to Calvary, and the actual crucifixion and death. Waters ends the scene with a final dig, a shot of an addict shooting up on the church altar.

Divine comes home to find her boyfriend (David Lochary) cavorting with a wayward girl (Mary Vivian Pearce). In a rage, she kills them and, in a scene featuring Waters's soon-to-be-trademark graphic "realism," dismembers them and devours their entrails. Now completely deranged, Divine launches into a ranting monologue, announcing her plan to kill various public figures (Ronald Reagan, Barbra Streisand, and Tricia Nixon), and raving into a mirror: "I love you. You're still the most beautiful woman in the world. And now, you're a maniac." In the end, she is raped by a giant lobster, and after surviving that ordeal, is finally gunned down by the National Guard.

1972

Pink Flamingos: Shot in 16-mm color on a budget of about $10,000, this was to become Waters's most famous film, and the one that truly launched his career. The theme of the gang as family (initiated in *Multiple Maniacs* and carried through *Cry-Baby*) is first truly explored in this ninety-three-minute film, later released by New Line Cinema in 35-mm, and starring the usual Waters gang: Divine, David Lochary, Mary Vivian Pearce, Mink Stole, and Edith Massey.

The story revolves around a bitter war between rival gangs. Divine and her group are universally known as the "Filthiest People Alive." Destitute, Divine lives in a pink and gray trailer with her son Crackers, her mother (Edith Massey—a bizarrely decrepit, yet sweet older woman introduced in *Multiple Maniacs*) and her "traveling com-

Flyer for the "gala world premiere" of Pink Flamingos in Baltimore.

panion." Edie abides permanently in an infant's playpen, dressed in a girdle; her entire existence revolves around eggs and she greets each day awaiting the arrival of the Egg Man. Crackers's girlfriend is Cookie; in one scene they make love with a live chicken between them. The Nelson family it's not. But these are the good guys.

The bad guys are Connie and Raymond Marble, Mink Stole and David Lochary in their greatest roles, playing a husband-and-wife team with genuinely bad taste in clothes and home decoration. The Marbles make their fortune by kidnapping young girls, artificially inseminating them with their servant Channing's sperm, using a turkey baster, and selling the babies to lesbian couples. They keep the girls in subhuman conditions until they either die or give birth. The Marbles covet the "Filthiest People Alive" title in the worst way.

Connie and Raymond mount a campaign of harassment: minor stuff, really, like mailing Divine a turd. Divine throws a birthday party, which features cheerful group cannibalism and a man who can sing through his anus. But the Marbles call the police, posing as shocked neighbors; while the Divine gang is away, the Marbles burn down the trailer.

Divine retaliates by "sliming" (licking) the interior of the Marbles' house, and after performing fellatio on her son, frees the slaves in the cellar—one of whom castrates and kills Channing in revenge.

Finally, Divine and her cronies kill the Marbles. Their filthiness title preserved, they decide to move to the Midwest to start fresh. And then, of course, comes the famous coda—wherein Divine follows a small dog out for a walk, and when it defecates, reaches down, scoops up the poop, and eats it.

1974

Female Trouble: Shot in 16-mm color, and released by New Line Cinema in 35-mm, this ninety-two-minute film was made with a relatively higher budget than *Pink Flamingos*, and starred Waters's by-now familiar stock company. While light years away from the production values of *Hairspray* and *Cry-Baby*, the film was Waters's most polished and elaborate yet.

The complex film is divided into five sections, presenting phases in the life of Dawn Davenport, perhaps Divine's most fully developed character. We see her go from troubled teenager to prostitute and petty criminal to full-fledged maniac. Though the film's tone is comic and

satirical, her story is so tragic and disturbing that it is difficult not to
feel sympathy for her, even as she engages in "anti-social" behavior,
including graphic if absurdly extremist child abuse (frequently chain-
ing her daughter to her bed and beating her with a TV antenna). The
comic story of Dawn Davenport unfolds irreverently, yet her experience embraces every conceivable travail of modern womanhood.

The convoluted, wildly inventive plot includes the usual assort-
ment of murders, rapes and kinky sex acts, as well as some of Waters's
most memorable scenes: Divine (in a brilliantly innovative dual role)
ravaging—and impregnating—the teenage runaway Dawn in a
garbage dump; the straight hairdresser Gator, Dawn's eventual husband, jousting with his tacky Aunt Ida (Edith Massey in peekaboo
leather outfits that must be seen to be believed), who nags him to turn
gay: "The world of heterosexuals is a sick and boring life"; Dawn walking down the aisle in a see-through white dress, "naked" underneath
(Divine wore a "cheater," or fake vagina, for these occasions).

But *Female Trouble* is nearly stolen by Donald and Donna Dasher
(David Lochary and Mary Vivian Pearce), the sick, fascistic beauty
shop owners who transform Dawn into the first crime model ("Our
experiment involves beauty and crime: you see, we feel them to be
one," says Donna). The Dashers ruthlessly exploit Dawn's mad desire
to be a famous criminal. After Ida splashes Dawn's face with acid,
in retaliation for driving Gator away, the Dashers take her picture
and tell her she's beautiful as she writhes in agony. In the hospital,
Dawn unveils her monstrous new face to her friends, who applaud
as if at an art opening.

The Dashers develop a new grotesque look for Dawn, with shaved
head and huge, peaked eyebrows. They inject her with liquid eyelin-
er, shouting "Model, model!" This is a reprise of the *Eat Your Makeup*
theme, exaggerating the way fashion and style are used to manipulate
women into accepting otherwise painful existences, as well as a spoof
on the emptiness of celebrity.

The stage show near the end of *Female Trouble* is one of the great
showpieces in film history. Dawn, dressed in a white ruffled jumpsuit,
cavorts wildly in front of an adoring audience, makes a speech glori-
fying celebrity whatever the cost, and starts shooting into the crowd.

Betrayed by the Dashers at the subsequent trial, she is sentenced
to be executed: the greatest possible accolade in her line of work. Dawn
has achieved fame, making it all worthwhile. She goes willingly to the

electric chair, giving an Academy Award-style thank-you speech. Her final words to an ungrateful and unaccepting world: "Please remember, I love every fucking one of you."

1977

Desperate Living: Filmed in 16-mm color and released in 35-mm by New Line Cinema, this ninety-minute film is (after *Hag in a Black Leather Jacket*) the only one that Waters made without Divine—who was acting in a play at the time—while the actor was alive. But the familiar faces include Mink Stole, Edith Massey and Mary Vivian Pearce.

Desperate Living is, in Waters's own words, his "least joyous" film, and its raunchily violent obscenity may be unparalleled in modern cinematic history; it is also full of marvelous stinging digs at nearly every level of society, from hippies and homosexuals to kings and politicians. The film is a revisionist fairy tale, featuring strong doses of lesbianism, perversion, and political despotism.

Mad housewife Peggy Gravel (Mink Stole) has just been released from a mental hospital. She rants and raves at her family, as her four hundred-pound black maid Grizelda (Jean Hill) tries to comfort her with "fit" medicine—and herself with the family's vodka. The husband catches Grizelda and fires her; he also searches her bag, finding his savings passbook and lottery ticket. When Peggy comes in screaming, Grizelda sits on the husband and smothers him to death. The two women escape in Peggy's Mercedes.

The fugitives are caught by a perverted policeman who tells them about a place called Mortville where people go who are ashamed of their crimes. Before releasing them, he strips and forces the women to surrender their panties, which he puts on. He propositions them with great subtlety: "I'd like to stick my whole head in your mouth and let you suck out my eyeballs." Writhing on the ground, he points the way to Mortville.

They arrive in the desolate town, its mud streets and shanty houses filled with derelicts, hippies, and boys in black leather. The two women find a hotel run by a tough lesbian wrestler named Mole McHenry (Susan Lowe) and her over-sexed middle-aged girlfriend, Muffy St. Jacques—burlesque queen Liz Renay in Waters's first celebrity guest role. They pay for the room, still occupied by the dead former tenant, with Peggy's late husband's lottery ticket. Muffy and Mole explain how they came to Mortville (in typically demented fashion).

That night, the happy hotel reverberates with the sounds of love.

Mortville is run by Queen Carlotta (played with delicious depravity by Edith Massey), a cruel despot. Her leather boy goons bring Peggy and Grizelda to the castle, filled with portraits of Hitler, Idi Amin, and Charles Manson. Carlotta explains that in Mortville, everyone must live in constant mortification; the Queen is not responsible for their welfare or happiness, only her own amusement. Peggy and Grizelda are forced to eat cockroaches, then hauled off for "ugly" treatments.

Queen Carlotta has declared the following day Backwards Day: everyone must walk and dress backwards. The four women walk backwards to a nudist camp, looking for a newspaper to check the lottery winner. At the camp, Carlotta's daughter Princess Coo-Coo shows up to coo at Herbert, the janitor her mother has forbidden her to marry (his response: "Oh Coo-Coo, every piece of trash I picked up reminded me of you"). The royal goons show up and shoot Herbert. The four women head to an S & M lesbian dance bar. They finally find a paper, discover that Mole has the winning number, and return to the hotel where Coo-Coo has sought refuge.

Peggy and Grizelda argue over protecting the princess. The goons storm the hotel and Grizelda is crushed as it collapses, whereupon Peggy and Coo-Coo are brought to the castle in cages. Carlotta disowns Coo-Coo and praises Peggy, asking her to be the new princess and help her plot to poison the populace with rabies (in this case, brewed from rabid bat pus and rat urine).

Meanwhile, Mole claims the lottery money in Baltimore, buys gifts for Muffy and forces a Johns Hopkins doctor to give her a sex change operation at knife-point ("I want a wang and I want it now!"). Back home, Muffy is conversing with her breasts when Mole returns, proudly showing off her new (still bleeding) organ. But Muffy is nauseated, and forces Mole to castrate herself.

Peggy, dressed as a wicked witch, mixes rabies serum in a cauldron. Coo-Coo is injected with the vile concoction and ejected from the castle. Foaming at the mouth, Coo-Coo enlists Mole and Muffy's aid. They sneak up to the castle, surprise the goons in a gay orgy, and find the Queen and Peggy. Coo-Coo bites Carlotta, and Mole shoots turncoat Peggy.

Muffy is declared the new Queen. The townspeople show up for a wild and joyous celebration of Mortville's independence, a banquet featuring a roasted Carlotta on a huge platter, as Coo-Coo dies of rabies.

1981

Polyester: This was the director's first film to be developed with and financed by New Line Cinema; it was Waters's step up to the big time, shot in 35-mm with a $300,000 budget. It starred Divine, Edith Massey, Mink Stole, David Samson, Mary Garlington—and Tab Hunter.

The film is another fractured fairy tale, with Edith Massey as a retarded fairy godmother named Cuddles. It targets a long list of Waters's pet subjects, including Catholicism, abused women, censorship, abortion, juvenile delinquents, the legion of decency, sex offenders, adultery, and the rich. The film tells the story of Francine Fishpaw, a kind and religious housewife who is pushed to the limit by everyone and everything around her. This is the flip side of *Female Trouble*, with Divine playing the mother of juvenile delinquents and the wife of a sadistic boorish slob. The film is probably best remembered for its inspired "Odorama" gimmick, scratch-and-sniff cards allowing the audience to share Francine's heightened sense of smell, as she sniffs her way through life's puzzlements.

The story begins as an angry mob gathers in front of Francine's house, protesting against her husband Elmer, who runs a local porno theater. Elmer is happy for the publicity, but Francine begs the crowd for forgiveness. We meet her daughter Lulu, a slut and a shoplifter, and her son Dexter, a foot fetishist who sniffs cleaning fluid. Francine is trying desperately to hold the family together and have a normal life.

She achieves her goal—after severe yet riotous trials and tribulations. Elmer leaves Francine for his secretary, taking every opportunity to taunt and humiliate her in public. Dexter turns out to be the odious "Baltimore Foot Stomper," long sought by the police as the scourge of foot-sore housewives. Lulu is knocked up by her thuggish boyfriend and tries to abort herself. Francine finally discovers true love in the arms of dreamboat Todd Tomorrow (Hunter), only to discover it's part of a plot he and her mother cooked up to defraud her. But Cuddles saves the day; Francine is reunited with her now repentant, rehabilitated children, and this time they really do live happily ever after.

1988

Hairspray: After a long hiatus, Waters reemerged with this 35-mm, ninety-minute film, rated PG and released by New Line Cinema. This film finally put Waters in the mainstream. It was also, sadly, Divine's last film role, as a warm and loving mother to newcomer Ricki Lake. The film featured a bevy of celebrities, including Sonny Bono, Deborah Harry, Ric Ocasek, Pia Zadora, Jerry Stiller, Ruth Brown, Mink Stole and a special appearance by Waters. Set in the early sixties, it follows an overweight teenager who becomes the queen of Baltimore as a regular on the "Corny Collins Show" (patterned after a Baltimore dance show similar to Dick Clark's "American Bandstand") and forces the producers to integrate the show.

Hairspray is the first Waters film to overtly treat a specific theme, segregation. Although the film has a musical story line, successful large-scale dance numbers, and the thread of lighthearted teenage romance, underlying all the action is the racism that prevailed in fifties Baltimore. But the film is also a joyously kitsch celebration of a bygone era, with scrupulous attention to period detail. The star cameos are uniformly hilarious, the highlight being Ric Ocasek and Pia Zadora's turns as a blitzed-out beatnik artist and a reefer-smoking bongo-playing poetess reciting Allen Ginsberg's *Howl*. Ricki Lake is delightful as Tracy Turnblad, the fat but limber heroine who dances up a storm, thanks to the innovations of her black friends. She triumphs over svelte but nasty former queen Amber and the prejudiced older generation, intergrating the "Corny Collins Show" with the help of her sidekick Penny, her doting mother/agent Divine and Motormouth Maybelle, black deejay and host of the segregated "Negro Night."

1990

Cry-Baby: Just as *Hairspray* spoofed the early sixties, *Cry-Baby* spoofs the fifties, particularly those teen musical romances that featured such stars of the day as Elvis Presley. Released by Universal Pictures, the film was developed by Imagine Entertainment and shot in 35-mm color with a star-studded cast, including Johnny Depp, Susan Tyrrell, Iggy Pop, Polly Bergen, Troy Donahue, Joey Heatherton, Joe Dallesandro, David Nelson, former porn queen Traci Lords, Patricia Hearst, Stephen Mailer (Norman's son), Willem Dafoe, and Dreamland regulars Mink Stole, Mary Vivian Pearce and Susan Lowe.

Described in the Universal production notes as "the ultimate juvenile delinquent love story," *Cry-Baby* is essentially a Romeo and Juliet fable recounting the Baltimore rivalry between the Squares—the straight, suburban white kids who support Ike and Pat Boone—and the Drapes, a gang of local cool cats and chicks led by heartthrob tunester Cry-Baby

Walker (TV star Johnny Depp). Naturally, the "bad kids" are the heroes. Waters's answer to *West Side Story* is his first real musical (although *Hairspray* had big production dance numbers).

This is Waters's first film after Divine's death, and he refers to it as his first "boy" movie, i.e., with a male lead (in the role of a man). But the main conflict is that of Allison Vernon-Williams (newcomer Amy Locane), torn between her good-girl upbringing and her raging hormones when faced with Cry-Baby and his rockabilly music.

Allison, an orphan, lives with her rich grandmother, Mrs. Vernon-Williams, society's most upstanding matron. The essentially decent Cry-Baby is also an orphan; his father was the Alphabet Bomber, and his parents were both electrocuted. Allison is good, but she wants to be bad; Cry-Baby makes her swoon, while her boyfriend Baldwin (Stephen Mailer) is straight and boring.

The Drapes hang out at Turkey Point, a swimming hole and country bar run by Ramona Rickettes (Susan Tyrrell), Cry-Baby's grandmother, and Uncle Belvedere (Iggy Pop), old renegades who whip the kids into a frenzy as well as help care for his perpetually pregnant sister Pepper's two precocious children. Cry-Baby liberates Allison from a suffocatingly tasteful talent show and whisks her off on his motorcycle to Turkey Point for a dance. She is thrilled and allows the other girls to give her a "bad-girl beauty makeover."

Exhibiting suitable moral outrage, a jealous Baldwin leads the other Squares in an attack on the Drapes, burning Cry-Baby's bike. They all end up in court, where Allison is freed but Pepper's children are put up for adoption and Cry-Baby is sent to reform school. While Cry-Baby sings and dances his anguish, Allison, at home, drinks a glass of his tears—Waters' homage to his kinky consituency.

Meanwhile, Lenora, a Drape jealous of Allison, proclaims to the press that she is carrying Cry-Baby's child and they are to be married. Naturally, this information sends Allison back to Baldwin and the Squares. She agrees to marry Baldwin.

After Hatchet-Face's unsuccessful rescue attempt by helicopter and the liberation of Pepper's children from the orphanage, the Drapes, dressed in animal costumes, head to The Enchanted Forest, a new theme park, where Allison is singing. They explain the real situation and take her to the reform school, where she sings for Cry-Baby's release. The judge sets him free, after the intercession of a chastened Mrs. Vernon-Williams. Cry-Baby delivers a thank-you speech outside the prison to the Drapes and Squares, separated by a roll of barbed wire. But then Baldwin claims his grandfather pulled the switch on the Alphabet Bomber, and Cry-Baby challenges him to a chicken race, with each opponent tied to the top of a car.

In a final musical extravaganza, the race is on. Cry-Baby and Allison sing along, as Pepper gives birth in the back seat. Cry-Baby wins, the Square car crashes into a chicken coop, and Allison somersaults through the air into Cry-Baby's arms. They both shed a single tear (Cry-Baby's trademark).

175

Photograph and Illustration Credits

p.   6   Photograph copyright f-stop Fitzgerald 1992.

p. 13   From the John Waters collection.

p. 18   Divine (Glenn Milstead) publicity still.

p. 22   Photograph copyright f-stop Fitzgerald 1992.

p. 25   Copyright 1992 John Waters, Wesleyan University Cinema Archives.

p. 30   Copyright 1992 John Waters, Wesleyan University Cinema Archives.

p. 35   Copyright 1992 John Waters, Wesleyan University Cinema Archives.

p. 40   Copyright 1992 John Waters, Wesleyan University Cinema Archives.

p. 45   From the John Waters Archive, Wesleyan University Cinema Archives. Copyright Universal Studios 1992. Storyboard sketch by Mark Heath.

p. 51   Sketches by Vincent Peranio; copyright 1992, The John Waters Archive, Wesleyan University Cinema Archives.

p. 60   Photograph by Bruce Moore; copyright John Waters 1992.

p. 64   Photograph copyright 1992, Gerard Rondeau.

p. 70   Photograph by Lawrence Irvine; copyright John Waters 1992.

p. 77   Copyright John Waters 1992.

p. 82   Copyright John Waters 1992.

p. 89   Photograph by Greg Gorman; copyright Universal Studios 1992.

p. 95   Photograph by Henny Garfunkel; copyright Universal Studios 1992.

p.100   Copyright John Waters 1992.

p.107   Photograph by Henny Garfunkel; copyright 1992 Universal Studios.

p.114   Photograph by Steve Yaeger, copyright John Waters 1992.

p.119   Photograph by Larry Dean; copyright 1992 New Line Cinema.

p.124   Copyright 1992 John Waters.

p. 131   From the John Waters Collection; copyright New Line Cinema 1992.

p.134   Photograph copyright f-stop Fitzgerald 1992.

p.138   Photograph by Henny Garfunkel; copyright 1992 Universal Studios.

p. 141   Photograph by Henny Garfunkel; copyright 1992 New Line Cinema; Courtesy of the John Waters Archive, Wesleyan University Cinema Archives.

p.145   Photograph by Henny Garfunkel; Copyright New Line Cinema 1992; Courtesy the John Waters Archive, Wesleyan University Cinema Archives.

p.147   Photograph by Henny Garfunkel; Copyright 1992 Universal Studios; Courtesy The John Waters Archive, Wesleyan University Cinema Archives.

p. 151   Photograph by Henny Garfunkel, copyright 1992 New Line Cinema.

p.155   Photograph by Thorton Daniels.

p.158   Photograph copyright f-stop Fitzgerald 1992.

p.165   Copyright John Waters 1992.

p.175   Photograph copyright f-stop Fitzgerald 1992.